A HISTORY OF WOMEN
in the
CANADIAN MILITARY

BARBARA DUNDAS

A HISTORY OF WOMEN
in the
CANADIAN MILITARY

ART GLOBAL

Canadian Cataloguing in Publication Data

Dundas, Barbara, 1971–

A history of women in the Canadian military

Includes bibliographical references

ISBN 2-920718-79-7

1.Canada - Armed Forces - Women - History. 2. Women soldiers - Canada - History. 3. Women and the military - Canada - History. 4. Canada - Armed Forces - Women - Pictorial works. I. Title.

UB419.C2D86 2000   355'.0082'0971   C00-94846-0

Publisher: Ara Kermoyan

Project coordinators: Paul Lansey, André M. Levesque

Copy editor: Jane Broderick

End paper: Molly Lamb Bobak, 1922–
Basic Trainees Learning to Stand at Ease
Oil on canvas, 76.7 cm x 101.5 cm
CWM - 12010

Published by Editions Art Global and the Department of National Defence in co-operation with the Department of Public Works and Government Services Canada.

Art Global
384 Laurier Avenue West
Montreal, Quebec H2V 2K7 Canada
ISBN 2-920718-79-7

Art Global acknowledges the financial support of the Government of Canada, through the Book Publishing Industry Development Program, for its publishing activities.

Cet ouvrage a été publié simultanément en français sous le titre de :
Les Femmes dans le patrimoine militaire canadien
ISBN 2-920718-78-9

TABLE OF CONTENTS

ACKNOWLEDGEMENTS

The publication of this book is largely due to the support of Dr. Serge Bernier, Director of History and Heritage, and his desire to produce a popular history of women in the Canadian military in celebration of the Millennium.

Many currently serving and retired Canadian military women, directly or through friends, offered valuable advice, shared research or simply told me their stories. In particular I would like to thank Glynnis Elliott, Susan F. Beharriel, Sylvie Lemieux and Eva Martinez. Employees of National Defence Headquarters also answered my questions and provided me with the results of earlier research, often on short notice; Leesa Tanner and Mike Whitaker were especially helpful. No history can be written without the support of librarians, and I owe special thanks to Madeleine Lafleur-Lemire of the Directorate of History and Heritage.

Members of the Heritage Section of the Directorate of History and Heritage deserve special mention for their encouragement and ideas. Alana Lewis gave me access to the articles she found in *Sentinel* magazine, while Joni Yarascavitch shared her research into CWAC bands. Steve Gannon, a veritable fount of knowledge regarding dress issues and tradition in general, was always willing to offer advice or locate that crucial bit of information.

I must acknowledge and give special thanks to those who helped in the editing and translation of my draft, in particular Kevin Burns for his English-language editorial assistance, Pierre Desrosiers for his superb translation and Andrée Laprise for her French-language editorial assistance.

Acknowledgements must also go to André Levesque for shepherding the manuscript through the inevitable red tape and the staff at Art Global, who ably guided me through my first experience with publishing.

Finally, I wish to thank my family for always being supportive. In these last months they have responded to my many cancelled visits because of commitments to "my book" with kind words of encouragement. To my husband, Ken Reynolds, I offer a heartfelt "thanks" and a truthful "I couldn't have done it without you!"

Barbara Dundas
Ottawa
June 2000

PREFACE

This millennium book affirms the importance of Canadian women in our nation's military history. Beginning in 1885, their participation tells the story of a group whose energies, though constrained by social forces, were unlimited in loyalty and devotion. From the time of our first conflicts as a nation, they nursed the wounded, sick and dying in a capacity which then and now requires an unflinching sense of duty.

In the First and Second World Wars, women's efforts slowly won them esteem and recognition. Outside the military, women fished and farmed, worked in factories and machine shops. Inside our Armed Forces, their insistent desire to serve opened areas that had formerly been closed, and our nation became familiar with the fact of uniformed women in transport and communications, in administration, supply, medical and operational fields.

Today, women in the military are sailors, soldiers and air personnel, and the following pages trace their progress from subordinates and auxiliaries to full partners who bring their skills to challenging, often dangerous jobs in Canada and throughout the world. As Commander-in-Chief of the Canadian Armed Forces, I am sure that anyone who is interested in the ever-evolving role of women will deeply appreciate this book that chronicles an important part of their full and equal inclusion in our society and our national institutions.

Adrienne Clarkson
The Governor General of Canada

This book is dedicated
to all those women
who have served
or are serving
Canada's armed forces.

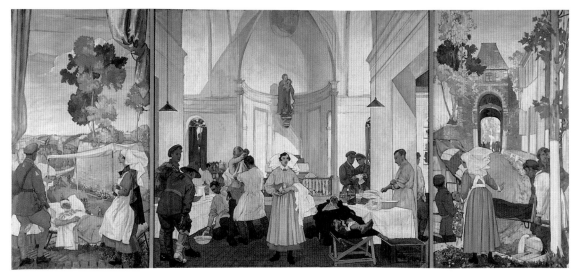

Gerald Edward Moira, 1867–1959
No. 3 Canadian Stationary Hospital at Doullens
Triptych. Oil on canvas
Canadian War Museum - 8555, 8556, 8557

INTRODUCTION

Courage, loyalty and devotion to duty in time of war, strife and emergency are qualities that Canadians have demonstrated throughout their history. The participation of women during such times extends back to the French and British colonial eras when, as civilians, they played an active role in the struggles leading up to Canadian nationhood. Some women are credited with acts of heroism in defence of their homes and families. In 1690, for example, Marie de Verchères defended her seigneury and its inhabitants against attack, as would her daughter, Madeleine, two years later. During the War of 1812 Laura Secord is said to have walked great distances through enemy-held territory to deliver vital military information about a planned American raid in Niagara. Secord's act of bravery would bring her lasting fame.

While such contributions by women are part of Canada's rich heritage, it is the story of women in uniform that is told in these pages.

During Canada's early military history, it was through nursing work that women exerted their greatest influence. The nursing tradition formed the basis for the first six decades of women's service with the armed forces of Canada. The soldiers who fought in the North-West Rebellion in 1885, the Yukon Field Force of 1898 and the three Canadian contingents that saw action in the South African War of 1899–1902 all benefited from the ministrations of Canada's nurses. A permanent Canadian Nursing Service was created in 1901, ensuring the continuity of this very important arm of the medical corps. Thirteen years later the First World War broke out. Canada was quick to respond to the call and once again its women rose to the occasion and volunteered for military duty, serving in hospitals in Britain, on the western front and elsewhere.

After the armistice was signed in 1918, just 21 years would elapse before the world was plunged into another global conflict and the role of women in the armed forces was necessarily expanded beyond the traditional one of nursing. By 1942 all three armed services had established organizations for women. These bodies were disbanded at the end of the Second World War, but the Korean War and the dawn of the Cold War era brought Canadian women into uniform once again. This time their organizations would endure, providing them with the opportunity to demonstrate that they could play an ongoing role in the military.

The succeeding decades witnessed an increase in the number of military occupations open to women. More recently, legislation to secure rights of equality for every member of society has brought about inevitable changes within the Canadian Forces, and in the past decade the Forces have moved towards full gender integration.

The year 2000 marks the 115th anniversary of the first response by Canadian women to their nation's call to service. The intervening years have seen triumph and tragedy, heroism and quiet duty, and the development of the tradition of service that is recorded in the following pages.

Nursing Sisters A.J. Attrill, RRC, E. Hudson, RRC, A. Howard and E.F. Wilson. (National Archives of Canada, PA 6827)

Chapter I

THE FIRST CANADIAN WOMEN IN UNIFORM: THE NURSING SERVICES, 1885–1918

The North-West Rebellion, 1885

Canadian women first answered their country's call to military service during the North-West Rebellion of 1885. Canada was still a young nation when it faced this second challenge to its authority from Louis Riel and his supporters, the same man who had incited the Red River Rebellion of 1869–70. In 1885 Riel again declared himself leader of a provisional government and demanded that Ottawa negotiate the terms of governance in its western territory. The federal government, however, had firmly established itself in the vast but underpopulated lands west of Ontario and, when word of rebellion reached Ottawa, ordered troops to the region. Most of

the journey was made on the nearly completed Canadian Pacific Railway, leaving only a relatively short, albeit arduous, distance to be covered on foot.

The Minister of Militia and Defence, Adolphe Caron, was confident of success but knew that, inevitably, there would be casualties. He accordingly ordered a medical contingent to accompany the expedition and appointed Lieutenant-Colonel Darby Bergin Medical Director-General for the operation. Bergin was the Member of Parliament for Cornwall, Ontario, the commanding officer of the 59th "Stormont" Battalion of Infantry and a surgeon. From the outset, he recognized the need for women nurses even though the scope of their involvement was not clearly defined. Canadians had learned lessons from the example set by Florence Nightingale in the Crimea three decades earlier, but in 1885 there was no organized corps of military nurses from which to draw. Instead, the government invited women across Canada "to form Red Cross Societies for the purpose of supplying medical comforts such as meat extracts, meat teas, jellied fruits and other comforts not on the diet roll of the Hospitals" — for example, shirts, bandages and medical dressings. However, Bergin suggested that as a contingency measure some members of these Societies might, if required, be persuaded to volunteer as nurses. Women across Canada quickly responded to this plea and a number received a letter of acknowledgement indicating that "should unfortunately the occasion arise for your services, [Minister Caron] will very gratefully accept them."

Lieutenant-Colonel Bergin gave careful thought to the potential role and deployment of an organization of military nurses, including the appointment of a superintendent-general to direct it. This person would be responsible for enforcing discipline and ensuring that the orders of the surgeon-major and medical officers attached to field hospitals were obeyed. In addition, Bergin stipulated that each nurse was to care for no more than 20 patients. However, a superintendent-general of nurses was never appointed and in 1885, in spite of the recommended quota, military nurses had to care for as many patients as required their attention.

Operational plans for the North-West campaign, like those of all military operations, were subject to change as circumstances demanded. While Bergin was contemplating the creation of a corps of nurses, two fully equipped field hospitals were sent west by rail. The hospitals were desperately needed after a force commanded by Major-General Frederick D. Middleton had confronted a Métis force led by Gabriel Dumont at Fish Lake on 24 April 1885, sustaining more than 50 casualties. These unfortunates were sent to a temporary hospital established at Saskatoon, then a small community just two years old. The hospital had limited resources and no trained nurses, although local women cared for the wounded as best they could.

The need for skilled medical assistance was apparent, and Loretta Miller, head nurse at the Winnipeg General Hospital, was called to serve. Travelling by train and cart, she arrived at the Saskatoon Field Hospital on 12 May and immediately took charge of the wounded. Two days later an engagement at Batoche resulted in a further 37 casualties and Nurse Miller soon had under her care more than 80 patients — soldiers, Métis and native Canadians — far exceeding the limit of 20 patients per nurse recommended by Bergin.

Loretta Miller was not alone for long. On 23 May she was joined by four assistants: Matilda Elking, Bessie Hamilton, Phoebe Parsons and Margaret Morris (Parsons was described as "assistant," Morris as "helper"). A week later, seven others arrived at a second field hospital established at Moose Jaw. This group comprised three trained nurses in civilian practice, Florence Cottle, Mary Mackenzie and Joan Matheson, and four nurses from the Sisterhood of St. John the Divine in Toronto — the Mother Superior of the order, Hannah Grier Coome, two postulants, Helen A. Church and Helena Frances, and a novice, Amelia E. Hare.

In addition to their medical duties, the nurses who participated in the North-West campaign were expected to establish recreation areas, make bandages, and distribute blankets, clothing and other supplies sent by various women's organizations and charities across Canada. When military operations were successfully concluded within a month of their arrival, their services were no longer required. The five nurses from the Saskatoon Field Hospital, along with the rest of the medical staff, accompanied the wounded to Winnipeg where their patients received additional medical attention.

Major-General John W. Laurie, the officer responsible for the lines of communication during operations in North-West Canada, thanked the nursing sisters for their contribution in a brigade order issued 26 June 1885. In particular, Laurie noted that it was

most satisfactory to have received the proof that those who have left their homes at their country's call have not been forgotten by the gentler sex, but that the ladies of Canada who have been so worthily represented by the party of nursing sisters who are now returning at the conclusion of their self-imposed duty have given all practical evidence of their willingness to share the privations & possibly the dangers inseparable from hospital work on active service...& on behalf of his comrades the Major-General tenders them sincere and hearty thanks.

Dr. Thomas G. Roddick, chief medical officer in the field, believed that the contribution of the nurses had been extremely useful. He had special praise for Loretta Miller, declaring that "much of the success which attended the treatment of our wounded at Saskatoon was undoubtedly due to the skill, kindness and untiring devotion of Nurse Miller." All 12 of the nursing sisters who saw service in the rebellion were awarded the campaign medal, inscribed "North-West Canada, 1885."

The Yukon Field Force, 1898

On 17 August 1896 George Washington Carmack and his native brothers-in-law, Skookum Jim Mason and Tagish Charley, discovered gold in a tributary of the Klondike River in the Yukon Territory. Within a year, more than 100,000 prospectors were trekking into Canada's northwest, unfortunately bringing with them more than dreams for a brighter future. The Klondike quickly became synonymous with danger and crime, and in the spring of 1898 a contingent of two hundred soldiers was dispatched to the Yukon Territory to assist the North West Mounted Police in bringing law and order to the gold fields.

No military medical component was planned for the Yukon Field Force, but the expedition was accompanied by four members of the Victorian Order of Nurses who were already bound for the area. Lady Aberdeen, wife of Canada's Governor-General, had established the VON the previous year to commemorate Queen Victoria's Diamond Jubilee. Her intent was to provide nursing care for people in isolated areas, and the Yukon expedition gave four members of the order — Georgina Powell from New Brunswick, Margaret Payson from Nova Scotia, Rachel Hanna from Ontario and Amy Scott, an immigrant from Great Britain who had been nursing in Ontario — ample opportunity to carry out such work. Consideration had to be given to dress, since the conditions of travel and life in the far north required clothing markedly different from that worn by most civilian nurses. The four women were issued uniforms made of durable cloth and resembling a bicycle suit of the period — complete with bloomers and a short skirt.

Throughout the long journey north the women provided medical care to the soldiers of the Field Force and occasionally to civilians who presented themselves. After spending some time at Fort Selkirk with the troops, they moved on to Dawson, their ultimate destination, where they nursed the civilian population while continuing to provide medical aid for military personnel. Although they were never formally part of the military, these women nonetheless made a significant contribution. In a letter to Lady Aberdeen, Lieutenant-Colonel Thomas D. Evans, commander of the Yukon Field Force, praised the work of her VON nurses: "Their presence with the Force has been invaluable, as scattered as it has been for the last three months over a distance of nearly 600 miles. I don't know how we should have fared without them."

The Yukon experience would prove to be particularly valuable for one of these pioneering nurses. Amy Scott, who was lauded by the assistant surgeon to the North West Mounted Police for her "untiring devotion," later served with the Canadian military not only in South Africa but also, at the age of 48, as one of the first hundred nurses dispatched overseas during the First World War.

The South African War, 1899–1902

In the summer of 1899 tensions in southern Africa between the British Cape Colony and the two Boer republics of Transvaal and the Orange Free State escalated into outright hostilities. The Canadian Parliament voted to support the British cause in July of that year, but, when asked in October to pledge soldiers for the war, Prime Minister Sir Wilfrid Laurier balked. After

political negotiation, a compromise was reached: a military force would be sent at Canada's expense but Britain would absorb the costs once the force arrived in South Africa. In keeping with this commitment, the Canadian government sent a telegram on 19 October 1899 offering the services of medical officers and nurses.

The British Secretary of State for War accepted the offer but stipulated that only British-registered medical staff, including nurses, would be permitted to care for British army personnel. This directive would cause minor tension between the nurses of the two nations until the war increased in ferocity and more and more trained military nurses were needed, requiring that the restriction be lifted. While many nurses applied, only four were selected to join the first Canadian contingent. On 30 October 1899 the first women to serve overseas set sail with the 2nd (Special Service) Battalion, the Royal Canadian Regiment of Infantry (RCR), aboard SS *Sardinia*. These were Minnie Affleck from Ontario, Sarah Forbes from Nova Scotia, Georgina Fane Pope from Prince Edward Island and Elizabeth Russell from Ontario. Russell had the advantage of previous wartime nursing experience, having served on a hospital ship during the Spanish-American War.

After an arduous journey of more than a month, the first group of nurses arrived in Cape Town only to discover that the RCR was to proceed "up country" without them. Georgina Pope recorded that although she and her colleagues "made every effort to be allowed to accompany them to the front,"

no nursing sisters can be accommodated in the field hospitals. So with very sad feelings we saw our countrymen entrain without us on December 3rd, and realized at that early date what served us in good stead later, viz, that we too were soldiers to do as we were told and go where we were sent.

The four nurses were placed under the authority of the principal medical officer of the British forces and sent to Wynberg, a short distance from Cape Town. They were later stationed at Rondesbosch, Springfontein, Pretoria and Kroonstad. Although they did not serve with the Canadian field hospital, the four women did get to nurse the occasional Canadian patient. Pope recalled that "as each new convoy arrived we eagerly searched for wearers of the maple leaf badge, and deemed it a great privilege to find them our own special patients."

The nurses sent to South Africa, unlike those who had served in the North-West campaign, were issued a uniform. Made of khaki, it "consisted of a short bicycle skirt worn with a Russian-type blouse equipped with shoulder straps and service buttons." They wore either a khaki hat or the English nursing cap, along with an apron and bib.

In December 1899 the government offered a second military contingent for South Africa, including additional nursing sisters. Of the 190 women who volunteered, once again only four were selected to accompany the Royal Canadian Field Artillery when it set sail from Halifax on 21 January 1900 aboard SS *Laurentian*. This second group of women, from Quebec, Ontario and Saskatchewan, consisted of Margaret L. Horne, Deborah Hurcomb, Margaret C. Macdonald and Marcella P. Richardson. Like Elizabeth Russell, Margaret Macdonald had served on a hospital ship during the Spanish-American War; she was destined to remain with the Canadian military for another two decades,

Miss Minnie Affleck, Nursing Sister, First Canadian Contingent, South Africa, circa 1900. (NAC, C 28733)

ultimately rising to the rank of Matron-in-Chief of the Canadian Nursing Service during the First World War.

This group of four was posted to Kimberley, Bloemfontein and Pretoria. Poor hygiene resulted in widespread disease among the soldiers, and at Kimberley the nurses tended patients suffering not only from wounds but also from dysentery and enteric fever. Horne, Hurcomb and Richardson fell ill, Horne so severely that she was forced to return home.

After nearly a year in South Africa, the women of the first contingent were ordered back to Canada in November 1900. Their homeward journey was intended to include a stopover in London so that Georgina Pope could receive, from Queen Victoria, the Royal Red Cross for "conspicuous service in the field." Unfortunately a broken railway line prevented them from sailing at the appointed time and compelled them to remain in South Africa an extra month. They finally made the journey to Canada in the company of the women of the second group, all seven arriving in Halifax on 8 January 1901. Georgina Pope did eventually receive the Royal Red Cross — the first Canadian to be thus honoured.

While Canadian women were serving as nurses in South Africa, their government was attempting to define their place in the military structure. Militia Order No. 20, of 25 January 1900, stated that nursing sisters were to be "accredited as Lieutenants with the pay and allowance of that rank." This accreditation of rank to nurses was far in advance of the practice in the British army, where nursing sisters were auxiliary civilian personnel with no rank or status. This led to some friction when Canadian and British nurses were stationed together.

In 1902 Canada offered a third contingent for South Africa, plus a field hospital (10th Canadian Field Hospital) and five nurses. This offer was accepted, but before this third group could be dispatched overseas some political wrangling took place. The British had requested five nurses, and the Canadian military authorities had selected the five when Frederick W. Borden, Minister of Militia and Defence, learned that Georgina Pope had volunteered for a second tour of duty in South Africa. The Governor-General, the Earl of Minto, did not want to increase the number of nurses. Borden therefore proposed that Pope be substituted for one of the five women chosen. Unfortunately, however, the

names of the original five had been released to the press and a last-minute change would result in a loss of face for the nurses and the government. After a considerable exchange of correspondence, Minto agreed to increase the number of nursing sisters and Sister Georgina Pope and two other applicants were added to the list.

Four of the women, Sarah Forbes, Deborah Hurcomb, Margaret Macdonald and Georgina Pope, had already been in South Africa, while Florence Cameron, F. Eleanor Fortescue, Amy W. Scott and Margaret Smith were going out for the first time. All were members of the newly established Canadian Nursing Service, which formed part of the army's medical services. Significantly, although the Canadian Nursing Service had just been created, they served in South Africa not as members of the Canadian army but in temporary Canadian units of the British army, as did all Canadian troops who campaigned in South Africa.

This third group sailed from Halifax on 28 January 1902 and arrived in Cape Town on 2 March. Lack of shipping space meant they were unable to accompany the men of the contingent and had to travel by way of Britain, prolonging an already lengthy voyage. Upon their arrival, the nursing sisters were again separated from the men of their contingent even though in this case the unit in question was a field hospital. They were posted to British No. 19 Stationary Hospital at Harrismith, caring for the large number of casualties incurred in recent heavy fighting.

Conditions in the field hospitals of South Africa were vastly different from those in civilian hospitals. In the field hospitals, set up under canvas, the nurses and their patients were subject to the whims of the weather, be

Members of the St. John Fusiliers' "Amazon Battalion," a paramilitary group sponsored and trained by the regiment during the South African War. (Private collection)

it sandstorms, rain or cold. Fresh water tended to be in short supply, and meals, prepared over an open fire by an orderly, were dependent on his skill and the prevailing climate. The nurses were made constantly aware of the war even in hospitals located far from the fighting. At Kroonstadt, for example, several 6-inch guns were placed within 46 metres of the camp. The staff "had prepared a 'donga' — a place of safety for helpless patients — and a bombproof shelter for all the hospital staff in case of attack, which for some time threatened daily." An even greater threat — and one greatly feared — was the plentiful population of scorpions and snakes that often entered the nurses' tents uninvited.

Enteric fever was still prevalent and Nursing Sister Hurcomb, still not completely recovered from the illness she had contracted during her earlier South African experience, was forced to return home. The other seven nurses remained in South Africa until after the signing of a peace agreement in May 1902. They left the hospital at Harrismith on 25 June and arrived in Halifax on 22 July 1902, bringing to a successful conclusion the first experiment in sending women overseas. In spite of the adverse conditions they had endured, Superintendent Pope later wrote that, for her and her colleagues, it had been "a great privilege to serve the Empire in assisting in caring for the sick and wounded in far away South Africa, and if we lessened their suffering as we endeavoured to do, we are amply repaid for the hardships which are necessarily encountered in such a campaign."

Creation of the Canadian Nursing Service

In 1901 the commander of the Canadian militia, Major-General Richard H. O'Grady-Haly, praised the work of the nurses who had accompanied the first two contingents to South Africa. Although few in number, he said, they "rendered good service, and did work no less creditable than the troops whom they went out to nurse." O'Grady-Haly voiced his support for the creation of a Canadian military nursing organization run by nurse veterans of the South African War.

When the Canadian Militia Army Medical Services was created on 20 May 1899, the establishment of a nursing organization had also been considered. The military had stopped short of making it a reality, but the wording of the formation order illustrates that they were aware of the need: "The creation of a Canadian Army Nursing Service in connection with the Military Base Hospital and Line of Communication is in contemplation, and will be organized at a future date." Before their intention could be made policy, Canadian women were ministering to the sick and wounded in South Africa.

On 1 August 1901 the Nursing Service was established, with eight of the first 10 nurses enrolled being veterans of the South African War. On 2 July 1904 a general order increased the number to 25 and decreed that nurses were "to be granted the relative rank of lieutenant with the pay and allowances of such rank, but in no case [is] their designation to be other than that of 'Nursing Sister,' and they are not to have any military command or authority." This designation was similar to that of dental surgeon and the two groups received the same rate of pay. The Canadian system contrasted with that of Britain: the British Army Nursing Service had been expanded in 1902 to form Queen Alexandra's Imperial Military Nursing Service, whose members were civilian employees of the army and possessed neither rank nor official military status.

Officers and nurses of No. 3 Casualty Clearing Station in front of the nursing sisters' mess, January 1919. (NAC, PA 3934)

Doctors and nurses of the medical corps at work in Operating Room No. 2, Halifax, circa 1900. (NAC, PA 28421)

The same general order of 1904 that increased the size of the Nursing Service also reorganized the army medical services into a regular component, designated the Permanent Active Militia Army Medical Corps, and a much larger reserve component, designated the Militia Army Medical Corps. The regular force medical corps and the nursing sisters who belonged to it were responsible for running military hospitals, instructing members of the reserve medical units and generally caring for the health of regular force personnel. The rules and regulations governing the nurses were largely based on those in force in Britain.

In 1907 the Director-General of Medical Services, Lieutenant-Colonel Guy C. Jones, proposed the creation of a nursing reserve. Many civilian nurses had, in fact, offered their services in time of war or emergency and would complement the roster of reserve doctors in existence. As a result, regulations were promulgated in 1910 to create an Army Nursing Reserve of women aged 23 to 45 volunteering for a period of five years. Nursing sisters, whether regular or reserve, were accepted only if they could provide proof of medical training. Every candidate was also required to

sign a declaration of her willingness, in case of war, to accept service in Canada or any other part of the Empire, in the former case under the regulations governing the Nursing Service of the Militia of Canada and in the latter under the Regulations of the Queen Alexandra's Imperial Military Nursing Service. Renewal of enlistment would be at the request of the member and at the discretion of a committee that was established to select qualified volunteers.

Dress regulations for nursing sisters issued in 1907 called for significant changes to their uniforms. The South African khaki clothing was replaced by a full-dress uniform consisting of a "waist and skirt of dark blue serge [and a] cape of scarlet cloth reaching to elbows." Adjustable white collar and cuffs, along with a white cap in an approved pattern and gilt buttons in the Army Medical Corps pattern, were also specified. For working dress, nurses wore a "waist and skirt of pale blue butchers linen," the same collar and cuffs as specified for full dress, and a white apron. This dress was completed with a "double-breasted overcoat of dark blue cloth and a dark-blue cloth headdress in the sailor pattern." Medals were to be worn on the scarlet cape and medal ribbons on the working dress.

Although military women were now in uniform, their numbers remained low. In 1911 the Militia Council reported that the regular force required nursing sisters at each military hospital to ensure proper patient care, and others to assist medical officers with the training of non-commissioned officers and men in nursing duties. As the storm clouds gathered in the summer of 1914, there were only five women in the regular force (one matron and four nursing sisters) and 57 nursing sisters in the reserve.

The First World War, 1914–19

Historians now generally regard the First World War as Canada's coming of age as a nation, yet for many Canadians alive at the outbreak of war in the summer of 1914 events in Europe seemed remote. "Partly the outcome, although there are other reasons, of the assassination of the Austrian heir to the throne and his wife," is how Ethel Chadwick, a young Ottawa diarist, summarized the 28 July 1914 Austro-Hungarian declaration of war on Serbia. Neither Chadwick nor anyone else could possibly have imagined in that long-ago summer that this new conflict would eventually cost the lives of more than 60,000 Canadian men and women and the wounding of almost 200,000 others. Although events in Europe may have seemed distant in the first days of August 1914, huge crowds gathered in cities across Canada to demonstrate their support for the Empire. While Canadian men volunteered for the army by the thousands, Canadian women also came forward to offer their services.

The "war to end all wars," as it would be termed, precipitated a major shift in long-held attitudes about the role of women in both military and civilian life. The handful of nurses in 1914 would have thought it highly unlikely they would be sent overseas, but the next five years were to change many beliefs. The nursing sisters serving and those who would be recruited later were professionals and, generally, middle-class. Although many Victorian ideas about the role of women in society still held sway in 1914, in Canada, perhaps more so than in Britain, the nursing profession was treated with great respect and a large percentage of nurses had had the benefit of a secondary education. They did not set out to challenge society's perceptions about the social roles of women, but their exemplary service in a long and costly war gave many people reason to rethink their ideas.

Nursing Sisters A.C. Andrew, RRC, S.M. Hoerner and J.C. Brady. (NAC, PA 6783)

Nurses seeing off the wounded from the capture of Hill 70 as they depart for "Blighty" (Great Britain), August 1917. (NAC, PA 1785)

The various motivations of these young women for joining up did not affect the ultimate value of their work. Some, like Nursing Sister Ina I. Grenville, followed fathers or brothers who had volunteered. Others admitted joining the Canadian Army Medical Corps because their husbands, fiancés or boyfriends were in the armed forces. Marjorie Saunders joined for this reason. Nonetheless, she recounts in *The Military Nurses of Canada,* "We made a contribution, we helped to restore so many to normal health. Nurses were valuable to the Army, we gave a different outlook to military patients, we braced them up and lifted their spirits; they depended on you so much." In the same book, Edna Williams confesses to enlisting out of curiosity, "to see what it was like." Ruby G. Peterkin thought it "worth coming to the war just to have been on the E11 [submarine]. You never pick up a magazine hardly but there is something about it and pictures of [decorated officers]."

The first wartime recruitment of nursing sisters resulted from Britain's request for a Canadian force to fight alongside the British army in France. This expeditionary force was to include a casualty clearing station, two stationary hospitals and two general hospitals. There was no shortage of candidates for the nursing component of these medical units, as thousands of women in both Canada and the United States wrote to the Canadian Nursing Service to volunteer. In Ottawa the head of the Service, Matron Margaret C. Macdonald, and her staff were kept busy acknowledging the applications and discussing the potential requirements with the various military districts across Canada. Candidates were interviewed and lists compiled of suitable women — and all this activity took place even before there were any official calls for nurses beyond the few already in uniform. The order to mobilize nurses was given on 16 September 1914. Shortly thereafter, a hundred applicants were ordered by telegram to report to Quebec City on 23 September.

The first women to arrive at Quebec City in September 1914 quickly learned how to fill out forms and join the ubiquitous queues for everything from vaccinations to uniforms. Uniforms were subject to close scrutiny since there was always the possibility that they would be too large, too small or flawed, perhaps with one sleeve longer than the other. When the first one hundred nurses boarded SS *Franconia* on 29 September 1914, some appeared at the dock with no official papers, just a telegram or telephone message. Many had received no military training. In this respect, those best prepared were the members of the reserve force, who had been required to attend a four- to six-week course of instruction at a garrison hospital in order to learn the routine of a military hospital and the duties of army nursing. A further handful had attended annual reserve summer camps and received additional training. Regardless of previous experience, all volunteers received lectures on military subjects and military nursing during the Atlantic voyage, although many would later observe that these lectures did not prepare them for the horrors they would shortly encounter.

This first group of newly minted women lieutenants arrived at Plymouth on 14 October 1914 amid enthusiastic cheers from large crowds on the busy docks and people aboard boats in the harbour. From Plymouth they travelled to London, where they were stationed at the nurses training school of St. Thomas' Hospital, founded in 1860 and supported by the Nightingale Fund. Canadian nursing sisters held Florence Nightingale in high regard for the professional standards set by "the lady with the lamp" in the Crimean War more than half a century earlier. The pioneer of military nursing served as an example of selfless devotion for the Canadians.

As this first group could not yet be employed in Canadian hospitals, Matron Macdonald arranged for some to be posted temporarily with British units. On 4 November 1914 Macdonald was appointed Matron-in-Chief of the Canadian Nursing Service with the relative rank of major, the first woman in the British Empire to attain such a rank. While they were in Great Britain the nursing sisters remained under Canadian control, but when they were eventually posted to units in France, Belgium, Greece and Egypt they came under the authority of the Matron-in-Chief, British Armies in the Field.

The first nurses arrived in France on 7 November 1914 as members of No. 2 Stationary Hospital. Following an uneventful Channel crossing, they had to wait three weeks for their hospital in France to be established before they could commence their duties. As soon as a suitable building had been located and the hospital set up, they got to work.

A number of the military hospitals set up during the First World War were closely allied

Personnel of No. 5 Canadian Stationary Hospital visiting the pyramids of Giza, Egypt, in 1915. (NAC, PA 122444)

to Canadian medical schools. Generally, the medical officers of the unit would be graduates of the particular university for which the hospital was named. As an example, No. 3 Canadian General Hospital (McGill) in France had many McGill University alumni on its original staff, including its second-in-command, Lieutenant-Colonel John McCrae, author of the famous poem "In Flanders Fields." No. 6 Canadian General Hospital (Laval) was staffed by francophone Canadians — its officers were graduates of Université Laval and its enlisted personnel were recruited in the province of Quebec. In August 1916, after a month in France, the

Medical staff and patients of "A" 2 Ward of No. 3 Casualty Clearing Station, July 1916. (NAC, PA 69)

majority of the male staff, all the nursing sisters and some 59 other ranks of No. 6 were transferred to other duties, while the equipment and the remainder of the personnel were transferred to the French military authorities.

Conditions were harsh for nursing sisters living "under canvas" near their hospitals. Ruby Peterkin described the bitterly cold winter in Salonika (Thessalonica, Greece) and the alterations she and her colleagues made to their uniforms to keep warm. Peterkin wore puttees for modesty as well as warmth, since the nurses had to hitch up their skirts to keep them clear of the snow and mud. She also "objected to showing the *whole* of [her] socks to the wide world." Field improvisation included wearing extra underclothes, flannel pyjamas, sweaters and other non-uniform articles of clothing such as gloves and even corduroy trousers bought locally or borrowed from officers. Peterkin remembered that some of the nursing sisters in the Dardanelles purchased riding outfits for both convenience and warmth.

Things were no better on the western front in France. Sophie Hoerner, stationed at No. 3 Canadian General Hospital, could never get warm. "The dampness goes to the very marrow of your bones," she reported, "and has I believe stopped [the] circulation in my feet," but "I am very well in spite of the dampness." These women would have welcomed the "bicycle suit" worn by the VON nurses who accompanied the Yukon Field Force.

In the face of these challenges, nursing sisters tried to make their tents as comfortable as possible, just as frontline soldiers did in their dugouts. These tents were, after all, used not only for sleeping but also for socializing,

Nursing sisters of No. 3 Casualty Clearing Station take advantage of the opportunity to have tea together, July 1916. (NAC, PA 74)

relaxing and letter writing. The nurses hung blankets against the sides of the tents to combat draughts and draped silk and other fabrics over their travel boxes to create a more attractive atmosphere. They acquired lamps, matting for their floors and storage boxes that doubled as furniture.

Discomfort was not the only problem. On 19 May 1918 No. 1 Canadian General Hospital was the target of a German air raid. Two nurses were killed and others wounded when the Sisters' Quarters received a direct hit. The matron and the nurses on duty never faltered during the attack and many off-duty nurses reported to the hospital to supplement their efforts. In a letter to the mother of Nursing Sister Katherine M. MacDonald, one of the women killed in the attack, the Minister of Militia and Defence wrote that the "heavy loss which you and the nation have sustained would indeed be depressing were it not redeemed by the knowledge that the brave comrade for whom we mourn performed her duties fearlessly and well as became a good soldier and gave her life for the great cause of Human liberty and the Defence of the Empire." On 27 June 1918 a submarine sank His Majesty's Hospital Ship *Llandovery Castle,* a vessel assigned to the Canadian forces, killing all 14 nursing sisters on board. In all, 43 nursing sisters lost their lives serving King and country.

The number of nurses wishing to join the Canadian Army Medical Corps always exceeded the number of positions available. By 1917 the number of sisters employed in Canada reached a peak of 527, while, over the course of the war, a total of 1,901 nursing sisters went overseas. An additional 313 women served with the British forces and many others joined the American medical corps, the Red Cross or other civilian organizations. A total of 328 decorations were awarded to Canadian nursing sisters for their efforts during the First World War, 50 of them by foreign governments.

After demobilization, many nurses maintained their military connections by working with federal organizations such as the Department of Re-establishment or with unofficial women's groups. Some of these groups, such as the Winnipeg Women's Volunteer Reserve and the Canadian Women's Emergency Corps No. 1 (Montreal), had been formed as early as 1915 and continued to function until the end of the war. Other women contributed to the cause through volunteer work at Maple Leaf Clubs for soldiers on leave, the Canadian Field Comforts Commission or other benevolent societies.

As the war progressed and the casualties increased, more and more men were draughted into the Allied armies. And as labour became scarce, women throughout the Western world suddenly found jobs and careers open to them that had been closed to them in peacetime. The Canadian government employed a large number of women in civilian jobs with the armed forces in Great Britain, France and Canada. In Great Britain some worked as drivers with the motor transport companies of the Canadian Army Service Corps, while others took jobs as clerks and stenographers. The personnel of Britain's Women's Legion and the Women's Army Auxiliary Corps (Queen Mary's Army Auxiliary Corps) were attached to the Canadian Forestry Corps and to Canadian medical units. During the winter of 1916–17 manpower shortages led the government to consider increasing the number of female

Nursing sisters with their bicycles during the First World War.
(Canadian Forces Photograph Unit, PMR 84-295)

employees in their overseas organizations to allow for the release of more men for combat duty. The government sought to employ members of the British Women's Army Auxiliary Corps or other British women abroad but was not interested in bringing Canadian women overseas.

Ironically, Britain's Royal Air Force (RAF) was employing Canadian women in Canada. By 1918 the RAF had engaged a large

A Canadian Volunteer Ambulance Division driver at the front in May 1917. (NAC, PA 1305)

number of civilian women as clerks and, despite local opposition, some as transport drivers. RAF Headquarters in Toronto was compelled by a shortage of staff to advertise an ever-wider range of jobs as open to women and eventually hired some 1,200, many in technical positions. By the end of the war nearly 750 women were working as mechanics for the RAF in Canada.

The widespread shortage of manpower and the need to release male military personnel for duty on the western front eventually led Canada's Militia Council to discuss the creation of a women's military corps based on Britain's Women's Army Auxiliary Corps. The concept was laid before an all-male sub-committee that included the Quartermaster-General, the Paymaster-General, the Judge Advocate General and a representative of the Adjutant-General's Branch. It unanimously recommended the establishment of an organization to be known initially as the Canadian Women's Corps.

Initial discussions established that members of the Canadian Women's Corps could fill such occupations as clerks, typists, accountants, librarians and shorthand typists. The subcommittee identified other jobs — cooks, mechanics and unskilled labourers — that might be assumed by women once the initial positions had been filled. The heads of the various military branches and the commanders of military districts across Canada were surveyed to determine the number of women already on the military payroll and the number who could take over positions then occupied by men. The results showed that 1,325 civilian women were employed as clerks, typists and shorthand typists, while 107 men were performing duties that could be handled by women. The subcommittee therefore recommended that currently employed civilian women whose work was deemed acceptable be invited to enlist. Those who declined were

A nurse receiving a dog that some wounded soldiers had brought out of the trenches with them in October 1916. (NAC, PA 984)

Nursing Sister Blanche Olive Lavallée departing for Europe during the First World War. (CFPU, PMR 86-344)

to be replaced by Corps members, and future appointees were to be drawn from the ranks of the Corps. Female members of the Permanent Civil Service were to be exempt.

At its 18 September 1918 meeting, the Militia Council approved in principle the formation of the Canadian Women's Army Auxiliary Corps and the Minister of Militia and Defence announced that he would discuss the matter with the Prime Minister. This decision was affirmed a week later but no evidence exists today to verify that the matter was ever pursued. The British Air Ministry and the Canadian government concurrently agreed to create a branch of the Women's Royal Air Force in Canada, but, as with the army, air force plans were overtaken by events.

Disembarkation of CWAC personnel at Naples, Italy, 22 June 1944.
(NAC, PA 108177)

Chapter II

SERVING THAT MEN MAY FIGHT:
THE SECOND WORLD WAR, 1939–45

The time now is the most crucial, momentous period of the War,
and it will be the help of those girls, the help of the women coming into
the Army, which will perhaps provide, so far as Canada is concerned –
the decisive impulse which may carry us to victory.

— J.L. Ralston, Minister of National Defence, 18 April 1944

We, the women of Canada, have claimed and procured the right to participate
through our vote in the direction of public affairs.
Today, we are taking a new step forward and we are asking our fathers,
husbands and brothers the favour of allowing us to stand next to them in
defending our country and our freedom. In this way, when the great day of victory
dawns, we may legitimately claim our share of the glory.

— *La Presse* (Montreal), 17 January 1942

The Interwar Period

At the end of the First World War, plans to have women serve with the army and air force were still in their infancy. In September 1918 it seemed likely that the need for a women's army corps would be brought before the Prime Minister, but no action was taken. Neither was the decision of the RAF to recruit women in Canada ever pursued, probably because of cost — estimates placed the per capita cost of housing women at $430 a year, compared to the $235 for men, the difference being attributed to the "necessity of special provision."

On the other hand, nursing sisters had proved their worth during the war and a small number were retained in the peacetime regular force and posted to military hospitals across Canada. The majority, however, returned to civilian life, many taking jobs with the Department of Re-establishment and joining organizations that would bring them into contact with other ex-military nurses. These groups, like male veterans' organizations, provided opportunities for friendship, volunteer work and political mobilization. During the Canadian visit of King George VI and Queen Elizabeth in 1939, the Overseas Nursing Sisters' Association was among the veterans' associations represented at the unveiling of the National War Memorial, and, notably, one nursing sister stood as a sentry during the ceremony.

During the interwar period the administration of the nursing service was handled by the Director-General of Medical Services, as there were no nurses posted to headquarters in Ottawa. The role of nurses in a future war was by no means neglected, however, and in 1927 the Canadian Nurses Association, with the approval of the Director-General and in cooperation with the Canadian Red Cross, established the National Enrolment Plan. Under this plan, nurses across Canada were contacted and encouraged to enlist in the reserve force for service in time of war or disaster. A number of nursing sisters attended summer training camps for the reserves and winter schools of instruction at regular force stations. This not only gave them an opportunity to qualify for commissions and promotions, but it also helped to develop a pool of trained military nurses who would be ready should their services be required.

Between 1919 and 1939 the number of military nurses varied from year to year. In November 1919 there were 27 military hospitals in Canada employing 377 nursing sisters, but as soldiers were transferred from military to civilian hospitals or released into civilian life the number of nursing sisters declined rapidly. The recently renamed Royal Canadian Army Medical Corps (RCAMC) was reduced to its pre-First World War strength, with fewer than 50 authorized officers. When the Second World War broke out in 1939, the regular force had one matron and 10 nursing sisters, while the reserve list comprised 331 nursing sisters.

The Coming of War, 1938–41

As tensions in Europe mounted, women organized volunteer groups in which to serve in the event of war. In the autumn of 1938, against the backdrop of the Munich Crisis, a group of women in British Columbia founded one such organization, the British Columbia Women's Service Corps (BCWSC). Its

A member of the CWAC examines a recruitment poster calling on women to serve "Shoulder to Shoulder," Ottawa, circa July 1942. (NAC, PA 128215)

members hoped that it would develop into an official women's auxiliary service of the Canadian army. In Britain, plans for the mobilization of women were more advanced: in September 1938 the British army created the Auxiliary Territorial Service; in April 1939 the British Admiralty established the Women's Royal Naval Service; and June 1939 saw the formation of the Women's Auxiliary Air Force.

These developments were closely monitored in Canada, and once Canada declared war against Germany, on 10 September 1939, many women wished to follow the example set in Great Britain and sign up. As there was no official government response at this time, patriotic women continued to form "paramilitary" groups across Canada. Among these were the Women's Voluntary Reserve Corps in Quebec, Ontario and the Maritimes; the Canadian Auxiliary Territorial Service, which operated in Ontario and the western provinces; and the Canadian Red Cross Corps, which operated across the country. French-speaking women founded the Corps de réserve national féminin and the Réserve canadienne féminine.

The women in these organizations sought and received training in skills such as motor mechanics, driving and small-arms handling. Some learned Morse Code signalling, quartermaster's duties and map reading, while others trained in more traditional women's work such as first aid and administration. These organizations adopted military-style accoutrements: some women wore arm bands with their civilian clothing while others wore complete uniforms — everything from regulation shoes to a service beret. The volunteer corps were organized along military lines and ranks were assigned. Training and uniforms were

paid for by the women themselves with no government subsidy, although a local reserve commander might occasionally authorize members of his unit to act as instructors. The Department of National Defence (DND) considered issuing warnings to groups whose uniforms, badges and ranks so resembled those of Canada's armed forces that they might imply membership in the military — an offence under the *Criminal Code* and the *Defence of Canada Regulations*. However, no action was taken and the real threat of confusion with members of the military did not arise until the army, navy and air force created their own women's organizations.

Determined to serve, the BCWSC asked the British War Office in July 1940 if recruits were needed for British women's organizations and if Canadian women would be permitted to join. The reply was that qualified personnel would be welcomed if they could provide their own transportation to Great Britain. Travel to Britain, however, was stymied by a Canadian government regulation stipulating that only members of the armed forces or civil service could enter European waters or the war zone around Great Britain. Many members of the women's paramilitary organizations, most notably Joan C. Kennedy, leader of the BCWSC, lobbied the government to sanction them as official auxiliaries to the Canadian forces or to establish a women's corps.

By the beginning of 1941 these corps had nearly seven thousand members across the country. A number of them organized a nationwide assessment of women's desire to enter military service and presented their findings to the government. However, the government resisted all attempts at persua-

Group of Canadian Red Cross ambulance drivers at De Haan, Belgium,
4 February 1945. (NAC, PA 128231)

Lieutenant B. Rankin, Royal Canadian Army Corps, administering a blood transfusion to a wounded soldier at Montreuil, France, 10 September 1944.
(NAC, PA 128234)

the military did not intend to assign to women. The announcement that a Canadian Women's Army Corps would be formed was nevertheless enthusiastically welcomed by the volunteer groups. An article in the *Vancouver Sun* on 27 June 1941 entitled "Women's Army Already Trained" reported that they were "practically in the army now...or at least that's the hope of Vancouver's uniformed women, following the announcement today that several thousand women are to be enlisted as an auxiliary corps to Canada's armed forces."

Canadian Women in the Military Medical Services, 1939–45

Royal Canadian Army Medical Corps

Although the RCAMC had only 11 regular force nurses in September 1939, this number was supplemented by the 331 women on the reserve list. The service expanded rapidly with the recruitment of nurses who were British subjects, under 45 years of age, unmarried or widowed without children and graduates of an accredited school of nursing. They were required to take a two-week qualifying course in procedures for military hospitals and methods of army nursing. This course was eventually broadened to include instruction common to all arms. Women skilled in other areas of medicine — dietitians, physiotherapists, occupational therapists and home sisters — were also recruited. All but the last group were highly trained professionals with full accreditation in their respective fields. Home sisters were not qualified to carry out nursing duties but assisted nursing officers by performing general tasks.

The uniform worn by members of the RCAMC Nursing Service during the Second

sion. Putting women in uniform might cause social disruption, it perceived, and was an ineffective way of spending the limited military budget.

As 1941 wore on, however, and the war escalated, Ottawa realized that women's desire to serve their country could no longer be denied. The government would have to act. It decided against endorsing any of the volunteer groups because of the "jealous claims" that would arise and because such endorsement might imply financial support for any new groups that might spring up. Another consideration was the fact that these organizations were training in functions that

World War differed only slightly from that worn in 1914–19. The satin lining of the greatcoat and cape was changed from scarlet to a more muted shade of cherry and the brass buttons on the greatcoat were replaced with black buttons.

The first RCAMC nurses to be posted overseas arrived in England in June 1940 as members of Nos. 5 and 15 general hospitals. By the end of that year 227 nursing sisters were on duty in England, and over the next five years many more would join them. After July 1943 some nurses were posted to active theatres of war. Nos. 5 and 15 general hospitals deployed first to Sicily and North Africa, respectively, facing the challenges posed by malaria in the former and weather in the latter. No 15 later moved to Italy and both hospitals followed 1st Canadian Corps on its campaign up the Italian peninsula. With the opening of the Northwest Europe theatre of operations in June 1944, more Canadian hospitals and nurses saw service on the continent.

Working so close to the front line, the nurses employed in the field hospitals sometimes came under fire. The very real dangers faced by military nurses are exemplified by the experiences of two women — Nursing Sisters Kathleen G. Christie of Toronto and Anna May Waters of Winnipeg, who were sent with medical personnel and nearly two thousand Canadian soldiers to the British colony of Hong Kong in October 1941. Action was not regarded as imminent

Nursing sisters of No. 10 Canadian General Hospital at Arromanches, France, 23 July 1944, including, L-R: Jean Scrimgeour, Susan Edwards, Neta Moore, Leona Whitmore, Margaret Stewart. (NAC, PA 108173)

and the soldiers were trained for garrison duty, not combat, but events unfortunately did not unfold as expected. In early December 1941 Japanese forces attacked the colony and on Christmas Day the Governor of Hong Kong surrendered. During the defence of the colony and after its surrender, the two nurses treated battle casualties but were eventually separated from the Canadian military prisoners and held in an internment camp with civilians until September 1943, when they were returned to Canada. Despite the hazards and hardships, they survived the experience and brought with them the first official information about what had happened to the Canadian forces in Hong Kong.

A total of 3,656 nursing sisters served in the RCAMC, 2,625 of them going overseas. Three hundred and ten nursing sisters were decorated: there were 111 Mentions-in-Despatches; 56 were made Members of the Royal Red Cross (1st Class) and 134 Associate of the Royal Red Cross (2nd Class); one RCAMC nursing sister received a King's Commendation and six received other foreign medals — one the Greek Distinguished Service Medal and five the Czechoslovakian Medal of Merit (First Class); also, one nursing sister was made Officer of the Order of the British Empire (OBE) and one a Member of the Order of the British Empire (MBE).

Royal Canadian Air Force Medical Branch and Nursing Service

Medical care for members of the Royal Canadian Air Force during the war was at first provided by the RCAMC, with a number of nurses being placed directly at the disposal of the air force. By the end of September 1940 there were 12 nurses serving at air stations; when the RCAF Medical Branch was created later that autumn they were invited to form the nucleus of the RCAF Nursing Service. All 12 accepted. Thereafter, women were recruited directly, and as the air force expanded — mainly through the increased number of flying schools — the need for nurses grew rapidly. Within six months of the formation of the air force Medical Branch the number of nurses had risen to 63, and in October 1944 the RCAF Nursing Service reached its peak strength of 395. Late in 1943 the air force began to recruit physiotherapists. Although a ceiling of 12 was set, only seven were appointed before war's end. Provision was also made for the appointment of occupational therapists but in the event the RCAF decided to use qualified civilian staff.

Given that the RCAF Nursing Service grew out of the RCAMC Nursing Service, it is not surprising that the uniform worn by these nursing sisters closely resembled the blue uniform of the RCAMC. The physiotherapists wore the same uniform as the registered nurses except that on the wards they used a cap instead of a veil.

For the first year, air force nurses held the relative rank of officer but were not accorded officer status. This caused some confusion and difficulty, especially in matters of discipline. A proposal to transfer the nursing sisters to the RCAF (Women's Division — WD) was rejected because the pay rate for nurses was higher than that for members of the Division. The nurses also argued that reporting to non-medical officers was not feasible and could result in a breach of their professional code of ethics. Resolution came in May 1942 in the form of a Privy Council order granting nursing sisters commissions on the same basis as their WD counterparts. For the sake of uniformity they were given the same ranks although they continued to be addressed as "Nursing Sister" or "Matron."

In November 1942 the Minister of National Defence for Air decreed that the nurses were to be granted the same ranks that applied to male officers. However, no order or authorization was published. The minister later stated that nurses would not be required to salute or return salutes, but some, including the Air Minister for Personnel, argued that this exemption would cause confusion for enlisted airwomen, in that they would have to salute some female officers and not others, and some officers would not be returning the compliment. In July 1943 a distinct rank structure for the Nursing Service was established, ranging from Nursing Sister (Provisional) to Matron-in-Chief, with equivalencies in pay and allowances to male officers on the non-flying list. The matter of saluting was not resolved until March of 1944 when orders stipulated that a nursing sister would salute and return salutes by making eye contact and bowing her head in the direction indicated.

Beginning in the summer of 1942, RCAF nurses were required to take a short course in aviation nursing, designed to train them in service organization and administration, essential procedures relating to air force medical work and general military nursing methods. In 1943 a small number of nurses were also given training in air evacuation in the United States.

The Service posted its members to most air stations and units across Canada and to British aviation training stations in North America. Sixty-eight air force nurses served overseas — 12 in Newfoundland and the remainder at or near RCAF stations and with No. 2 (RCAF) Mobile Field Hospital in Great Britain. Less than two weeks after D-Day, No. 2 (RCAF) Mobile Hospital, accompanied by two nurses, landed in Normandy. Nursing Sisters Davina Pitkethley and Dorothy Mulholland were the first Canadian servicewomen posted to France during the war. RCAF nursing sisters eventually served with the Mobile Field Hospital at Luneburg, Germany, and by 1945 found themselves deeper into German territory than any other Canadian nursing sisters.

Of the 481 nurses who served in the RCAF, 15 were decorated for their service during the war: one received a Mention-in-Despatches; one received the King's Commendation for valuable services in the air;

two were made Members of the Royal Red Cross (1st Class); and 11 were made Associates of the Royal Red Cross (2nd Class).

Mention should also be made of women medical officers in the RCAF. A shortage of professional medical staff in the air force was addressed by directly commissioning women doctors. In this regard the RCAF was ahead of the other services. The first female medical officer, Dr. Jean Davey, was appointed on 18 August 1941. Eventually 14 women medical officers served, most engaged in duties relating to WD personnel. The RCAF female medical officers carried the ranks of WD members but in other respects were equal members of the Medical Branch.

Royal Canadian Navy Nursing Service

Prior to 1941 the Royal Canadian Navy (RCN) did not have a system of hospitals, nor did it have any nurses. Personnel with minor illnesses or injuries were cared for by sick berth attendants in the Sick Bay — a sort of infirmary — of warships. More serious cases were treated at army and Department of Veterans' Affairs (DVA) hospitals. In the autumn of 1941 the first naval hospitals were established and the RCN Nursing Service was created. The first members were trained at army hospitals, but, as the number of naval hospitals increased, nursing sisters were trained within the naval medical system. In addition to naval medical procedure, they received instruction in general naval routine and some aspects of the duties of naval personnel, so that they would have a better understanding of their patient responsibilities and needs.

Candidates were required to be graduates of nursing schools associated with accredited hospitals and under 36 years of age, although some exceptions were made. Naval nurses were permitted to leave the service when they married but had to complete a year's service before receiving permission to marry. An abundance of potential recruits for the naval nursing service allowed the navy to select candidates from each province in numbers roughly proportionate to its population. The RCN Nursing Service also employed other qualified personnel — laboratory technicians, dietitians, physiotherapists, occupational therapists and home sisters. The requirement for physiotherapists and occupational therapists so far outstripped supply that some officers entered the navy directly from univer-

sity, fulfilling their internship requirement at a naval hospital under the supervision of a senior officer. These women, like the nursing sisters, had the status of male officers, holding equal rank within the navy. The term "Nursing Sister" was soon changed to "Nursing Officer" to reflect the diversity of tasks performed by the members.

The RCN Nursing Service was greatly influenced by the opinions of Colonel Elizabeth Smellie, Matron-in-Chief of the RCAMC Nursing Service, and it was on Smellie's advice that a uniform similar to that of the RCAMC was adopted. Naval nursing officers wore the straight gold lace rank insignia of the RCN with a maroon distinction cloth. Other medical trades wore a green cloth within the gold. All female officers wore "a close-fitting navy blue hat with officer's gold badge [and their] jacket is single breasted with belted back." On formal occasions they wore a navy blue silk dress with a stiff white collar and a flowing organdy veil.

The nursing officers played an important part in the training of male sick berth attendants, who served both in naval hospitals as orderlies and in ships as practical nurses caring for injured and ill sailors. Some members of the Women's Royal Canadian Naval Service (WRCNS) also trained as sick berth attendants but were employed only in hospitals and WRCNS Sick Bays. Nursing officers also served in the Special Treatment Centre for men of all three

Canadian nurses on board the *Lady Nelson* at Naples, Italy, 29 January 1944. (NAC, PA 163661)

services suffering from tuberculosis and in the Well Baby Clinics for the infants and pre-school children of naval personnel. They did not serve at sea. The only Canadian naval hospital overseas, HMCS *Niobe*, in Greenock, Scotland, was a coveted posting and naval nurses vied with each other to be sent there.

The only naval nurse to lose her life on service was Nursing Officer Agnes W. Wilkie, who was on board the ferry SS *Caribou* in 1942 when it was sunk off Newfoundland by a German submarine. The St. John's *Daily News* covered the circumstances of Wilkie's death as well as her funeral, with its full naval honours and the many military personnel in attendance: "Three volleys rang out and, as the notes of 'Last Post' died away in the stillness of the afternoon, Commodore E. Rollo Mainguy [Flag Officer Newfoundland] stepped up to the open grave and brought his right hand up in final salute." Dietitian Margaret Brooke, a fellow nursing officer, received an MBE for her attempt to save Wilkie's life.

From the first three nurses recruited in October 1941 and three RCAMC nurses "borrowed" to set up the service, the RCN Nursing Service grew to 345 officers before the end of the war, with 49 nursing officers serving in Great Britain. Honours awarded to members of the RCN Nursing Service included one MBE, six Members of the Royal Red Cross (1st Class) and 16 Associates of the Royal Red Cross (2nd Class).

Canadian Women in the South African Military Nursing Service, 1942–43

One of the little-known aspects of women's participation in the Second World War is the role of the South African Military Nursing Service. The difficulties and danger involved in evacuating the sick and injured from the battlefields of North Africa and getting them to Great Britain, as well as the fact that medical facilities in Britain were stretched and under constant threat of air raids, created a need for facilities on the African continent. The Union of South Africa took on the task but the number of casualties was too great for its military medical services to handle. In particular, there was a desperate shortage of nurses. The Canadian government therefore agreed to allow South Africa to recruit women in Canada. By July 1942 more than three hundred nurses had enrolled, 299 of them eventually serving as members of the South African Military Nursing Service at the expense of the government of South Africa, with minor financial contributions from the Canadian government.

Into Uniform: Creation of the Women's Organizations, 1940–41

In 1940 an anticipated shortage of male clerks and the perceived advantages of having female military clerks instead of civil servants caused DND to reconsider its earlier refusal to recruit women. Military clerks, it was believed, could easily be posted where they were needed, would be available for duty at any time and could be expected to take a "military point of view" resulting in higher standards. Military staff also believed — based on the enthusiasm demonstrated by the women's volunteer groups — that women wished "to exhibit and realize their part in the war effort." But military staff were also aware of the disadvantages: women would have to be provided with special accommodation, clothing, and medical and dental services.

CWAC personnel servicing a tank at the Longue Pointe Ordnance depot, Quebec, 20 April 1944.
(NAC, PA 128260)

On 2 April 1941 representatives from all three services met to discuss the issue of employing women in the Canadian armed forces. The RCN and RCAF considered such action unnecessary and unjustified. It would be another 13 months before the navy established a women's service. The air force, however, quickly changed its mind and within three months had started planning for a women's service. The government left the door open for each of the services to form women's organizations when it issued the following statement on 20 June 1941:

The government has now decided that, in view of the ever-increasing demands upon Canada's available man-power by the Armed Forces, war industries, agriculture and other essential occupations and services, including transportation and public utilities — Canadian women should now be organized to fill these positions. Among other things this will release considerable numbers of men already in the services, for combatant duties elsewhere.

Royal Canadian Air Force (Women's Division), 1941–45

The RCAF's decision to reverse its stand on the employment of women early in the summer of 1941 was the result of a growing manpower shortage and the decision of the British Air Ministry to employ members of Women's Auxiliary Air Force at RAF schools in Canada. On 2 July 1941 the Governor-General, the Earl of Athlone, authorized the creation of "a component of the RCAF to be known as the Canadian Women's Auxiliary Air Force, their function being to release for other duties those members of the RCAF presently employed in administrative, clerical and other comparable types of service employment." The British Air Ministry offered to send six Women's Auxiliary Air Force officers to help establish the Canadian organization, while Princess Alice, wife of the Governor-General, signed on as Honorary Air Commandant.

The use of the word "auxiliary" in the title implied that the women were not full members of the RCAF. They were, in fact, a component of the RCAF and were subject to air force regulations, with certain modifications. In view of this, Charles G. Power, Minister of National Defence for Air, asked the Privy Council to redesignate the new organization as "Royal Canadian Air Force (Women's Division)." The Governor-General formally approved the

Privates Vivian Dagleish, Betty Boan and Dora Silvester, members of the CWAC
Laundry Unit, at pressing and calendaring machine, Surrey County Council Central
Laundry, England, 19 August 1943. (NAC, PA 129090)

Airwoman 1st Class J.O. Malott sorting and filing correspondence at the Central
Registry, circa 1942. (CFPU, PL 9856)

change on 3 February 1942. The Judge Advocate General alerted Power to the lack of clarity under existing law as to whether WD officers could be granted and hold commissions. To remedy the situation the government declared, by Privy Council Order, that WD members selected as officers were granted, and did hold, commissions as officers of the RCAF, retroactive to 2 July 1941.

The RCAF (WD) was formed around a cadre of 150 women from coast to coast, selected by special committee. These recruits reported for a five-week administration course in Toronto, upon completion of which the first officers and NCOs were selected. After the first group was trained, the RCAF anticipated needing approximately two thousand women over the first five or six months. As "pioneers of the new Force," these women would "have special opportunities for advancement and should be smart and efficient." The air staff intended to draw all women officers from the ranks of enlisted personnel, but it became apparent from the experience of the first administration course that many of the most desirable officer candidates would not be leaving good positions unless assured of officer status. Therefore, some candidates received direct appointments as officers from a selection board.

The general qualifications for an airwoman were that the candidate be between the ages of 21 and 49, in good health, at least five feet tall and within the required weight standard. She had to have at least a "High School Entrance" standing, be able pass a trade test and be of "good character" — anyone who had been convicted of an indictable offence was ineligible. Women holding permanent positions within the civil service and those

who were married with "children dependent on them for care and upbringing" were also ineligible. This applied to women with dependents in general; exceptions could be made, but in such cases no dependent's allowance would be offered. As for the selection of officers: all other qualifications being equal, preference was given to candidates who had been officers in women's paramilitary organizations. Upon enlistment, women took an oath of allegiance and agreed to serve anywhere they were required.

At first, women were brought into the RCAF through the same recruiting centres as

Applicant Rosamund Fiddes being medically examined by Surgeon Lieutenant T.E. Wilson at the Joint Service Headquarters in Vancouver, 14 May 1943.
(CFPU, HN 415)

Members of the RCAF (WD) posted to No. 13 Service Flying Training School relax after a hard day on 21 March 1942. L-R: Margaret Daly, Florence Brisebois, Jean Steel, Ann Moyer, Florence Delaney. (NAC, PA 108268, Montreal *Gazette*)

Members of the WRCNS in their dormitory, Halifax, May 1943. (NAC, PA 128192)

Members of the RCAF (WD) "at home" in their barracks, circa 1942. (CFPU, PL 12061)

men. Since space limitations precluded separate rooms for interviews and medical examinations, certain times were reserved for the processing of female applicants. Because some women recruits were uncomfortable with the arrangements for medical examinations, registered nurses were called in to assist male doctors. As the number of women recruits grew, separate facilities were provided at the recruiting centres and, as time passed, WD officers and NCOs replaced their male counterparts in the interview process, thus alleviating any discomfort. Despite these attempts at accommodation, enlistment was generally handled in the same way as enlistment of male recruits.

WD members received two thirds the pay of RCAF officers and airmen, with an increase to four fifths in July 1943. Medical officers enlisted under the same terms as their male colleagues and were paid equally. Airwomen were also entitled to a rehabilita-

tion grant on the same basis as the men and, if serving overseas, were similarly exempt from income tax and the National Defence Tax. They were not able to assign dependent's allowances, however, nor were they entitled to such allowances while in uniform. Eventually, servicewomen were given the right to a separation allowance if married to a serviceman. A dependent's allowance for members of the WD was also later approved.

Air Vice-Marshal John A. Sully, in a memorandum to the Chief of Air Staff, argued that women and men carrying out the same duties should receive the same pay. He stated that while all airmen were theoretically liable to serve in combat, in reality many men were combatants in name only. Similarly, while all airmen could be obliged to fly, in practice many, such as ambulance drivers, never did, yet there was no suggestion of lowering their pay. Some women serving overseas were at greater risk than the airmen serving in Canada yet were not receiving equal pay. Finally, Sully contended that the low rates of pay for women contributed to recruiting problems. Nonetheless women continued to be paid 20 per cent less than their male counterparts for the duration of the war, although the extra pay given to specialists in a particular trade was the same for both sexes.

Women in the RCAF were bound by the same obligations and regulations as their male counterparts. They lived under similar conditions and worked in the same trades under the authority of the same officer, but their discipline and welfare were left to WD officers. Airwomen and their officers had a separate system of ranks, which parallelled that of the male members. They entered the service as aircraftwomen, 2nd class — the equivalent of aircraftmen 2nd class — and the most senior officer in the WD was a wing officer, the equivalent of a wing commander. Three women — Kathleen O. Walker, Winnifred Taylor and Kathleen L. Jeffs — attained this rank during the war.

As the Chief of Air Staff reminded all commands in 1943: "All officers, whether male or female, all other ranks whether airmen or airwomen, are subject to the same disciplinary regulations and exercise the same powers of command and punishment of the position held and the personnel under them. ...no difference exists between male and female members of the service." Female doctors and nurses proved the exception to this rule; these women served as members of the Medical Branch, rather than as WDs, and enjoyed no punitive powers. The application of discipline was in reality not equal, as women were never held in detention as punishment but instead received fines or extra duties. This difference in approach to discipline led, on occasion, to dissatisfaction among airmen. Some airwomen were aware of the more lenient treatment they received when it came to infractions — as one airwomen recalled, they could

"get away with a whole lot more than the boys could."

Airwomen were recruited into a choice of nine trades: "administrative; clerks, general and stenographic; cooks; transport drivers; equipment assistants; fabric workers; hospital assistants; telephone operators; and standard duties, which includes general duties and mess women." With so many women in clerical positions, it was sometimes difficult for them to see themselves as members of the military. As Ruth MacDonald recalled with regret, "It seemed like I wasn't in the Air Force at all. We were just like civilians in uniform." The decision to form women's components of the three services had been based on the need for administrative and clerical help, but it frustrated many of the more enthusiastic women in blue. Eventually

Members of the RCAF (WD) with their kit arranged on bunks for inspection, CFB Rockcliffe, 29 September 1942. (CFPU, PL 11449)

65 trades, out of a total of 102, were opened to women, but, because they were prohibited from taking on a combat role, women could not enter the aircrew trades such as pilot, navigator, wireless operator (air) and gunner. By 1943 trades courses open to both men and women were no longer segregated by sex. In January of that year the Minister of National Defence for Air submitted a proposal to the Cabinet War Committee that female pilots be employed for light flying duties. A decision on the proposal was deferred until the shortage of pilots became pressing, and this never came to pass.

Airwomen and their officers were generally pleased with their uniforms, which consisted of blue woollen tunic and skirt, blue shirt with collar, woollen stockings and black leather oxfords encased in black jersey overshoes. Windproof black leather gloves, a princess-styled greatcoat and a blue woollen cardigan were added for warmth. Fatigue clothing consisted of a blue broadcloth work dress, khaki combination overalls and blue canvas shoes. A khaki skirt and tunic along with khaki shirt with attached collar were worn during the summer. A black tie and brass collar pin were also included. Light-weight blue dresses were provided for wear on stations during the summer months. Regulations governing underclothing did not dictate type but did require the purchase of certain items, for which $15 upon enlistment and a quarterly allowance of $3 were provided. Airwomen who worked in motor transport sections and those serving under particularly harsh weather conditions were issued special warm clothing.

The first members of the WD to be posted overseas left Canada on 21 August 1942.

Over the course of the war, almost 17,000 women served with the RCAF (WD), including some 260 women from New-foundland, not yet a part of Canada. A further 328 women were recruited overseas. Fifty women were decorated for their service: 27 received Mentions-in-Despatches, one received an OBE and eight an MBE, and 14 received the British Empire Medal (BEM).

Canadian Women's Army Corps, 1941–45

The Canadian army had been considering the creation of some type of women's organization since the outbreak of war. A growing manpower shortage spurred the decision-makers to action and on 13 August 1941 the Canadian Women's Army Corps (CWAC) was officially formed, primarily for the purpose of releasing male soldiers "for more active duty." Since the CWAC was not part of the army proper, a separate system of ranks and a separate set of regulations and instructions were deemed necessary.

Unlike the navy and air force, which brought in British officers from equivalent services to guide the formation of their women's corps, the army relied on its own personnel and the experience gained by the members of the paramilitary groups. Matron-in-Chief Elizabeth Smellie of the RCAMC Nursing Service led the CWAC through its formative months. In early September 1941 she conducted a cross-country tour, meeting with the commanding officers of the military districts, prominent citizens and volunteer leaders in order to identify suitable candidates for the first administration course that would produce the officers and NCOs of the new service. Smellie described the regulations, assessed conditions in the locations where servicewomen might be employed and provided information on pay and uniforms. From the recommendations gathered on the tour, candidates were selected in each of the military districts across the country and 157 were instructed to report on or before 15 September 1941. Joan C. Kennedy, former leader of the BCWSC, was Smellie's first appointment. Kennedy's first posting was as the district CWAC officer in Military District No. 11, Victoria, British Columbia.

Military staff were soon proposing that the women's corps be made part of the active army so that "more effective control and supervision" could be exercised over its personnel and also to "facilitate uniformity in administration." The comparison between the status of the RCAF (WD) members and women in the army added to the pressure, and even the Judge Advocate General felt compelled to recommend that the CWAC be brought under the *Army Act*. J.L. Ralston, the Minister of National Defence, reminded his officials in a memorandum that unless it was, the CWAC's functioning in the army would require special regulations. Ralston ordered the change made unless there was a compelling reason to retain the status quo. Effective 1 March 1943, therefore, the CWAC was made part of the active militia (the wartime term for the mobilized regular army); all personnel who had enlisted up to that point were required to declare their willingness to serve as part of the army. The Order in Council changing the status of the CWAC also dictated that women officers would assume army rank and wear the equivalent badges of rank.

Officer candidates had to be physically fit British subjects between the ages of 21 and 55

having completed high school and possessing certain military qualifications that might be necessary from time to time. NCO candidates had to be physically fit British subjects between the ages of 21 and 40 having completed Grade 8 or the equivalent. Women with dependent children were ineligible. For all applicants, the minimum height and weight were set at five feet and 105 pounds; taller women had to be within 10 pounds of the standard height:weight ratio.

Female officers and enlisted personnel were considered junior to their counterparts in the army even when rank and seniority were equal. While male officers and NCOs in the army could hold power of command over CWAC personnel who were junior by rank, appointment or seniority, CWAC officers could only hold power of command over male officers and enlisted personnel who were placed specifically under their command. In the RCAF, in contrast, female officers enjoyed the same powers of command as male officers of equivalent rank.

The attitudes of male personnel greatly influenced women's view of service life. As recorded in *Greatcoats and Glamour Boots*, one officer found the prewar regular officers more difficult to deal with than those who had joined, as she had, "for the duration." The latter, she said, seemed much more willing to view military service "as if it were any other job we all had to do together, but the permanent force officers were just dreadful!" Corporal Ruth Tierney, in *Petticoat Warfare*, contrasts herself, "bursting with enthusiasm and a crusading spirit...young, eager and very gullible," with the officer to whom she reported. "On meeting the Major I found him to be fully bilingual and a brilliant leader of MEN," but he was not, she lamented, pleased to be dealing with women, nor very proficient at leading them. While the women were "serving that men may fight," they sometimes had to fight in order to serve!

Like the air force, the army initially offered women only two thirds the rate of men's pay. This discrepancy caused aggravation, although when the rate later rose to 80 per cent of men's pay most women were satisfied. As in the civilian workplace at this time, men and women were not paid equally. Trades pay for women, as described above, was less than that of men carrying out the same task until 24 July 1943, when equal rates were established. Command and staff pay rates for women were always equal to those for men.

At the outset, members of the CWAC were offered a relatively limited choice of trades, ranging from office work (accounting, stenography and clerical duties) to canteen or mess service and work in army stores. It was assumed that the women presenting themselves would be fully qualified. Thus there were no regulations in place to govern their training, beyond a general statement that district commanders were responsible for the training of recruits. The expectation of fully qualified recruits was soon shown to be unrealistic, however, and in October 1941 more elaborate plans were laid. A basic training syllabus was approved and made available in January 1942. The number of trades open to women grew as the year wore on, but as they became eligible for these traditionally male jobs the women would need more extensive training.

In February 1942 the CWAC leased Macdonald College at Sainte-Anne-de-Bellevue, Quebec, from McGill University for use as a training centre. On the 22nd of that month the first course of basic instruction commenced. Male officers and NCOs acted as instructors at first, but the CWAC soon provided its own teaching personnel. Training facilities continued to expand as the year progressed. Additional basic training centres were opened at a provincial agricultural college in Vermilion, Alberta, and at Kitchener, Ontario. Macdonald College, meanwhile, became the Advanced Training Centre. On 31 May 1944 the training centre at Vermilion closed and all training was concentrated in Kitchener. After basic and cadet training, some members took advanced training or NCO, warrant officer or regimental officer courses. Courses in chemical warfare and in instruction technique were also open to members.

While many women would later admit to being attracted to the army for the smartness of the uniform, at least one CWAC hopeful had strong reservations about the uniform being discussed over the summer of 1941. She appealed to Madame Thérèse Casgrain, President of the Quebec League for Women's Rights (and wife of Secretary of State P.F. Casgrain): "I do hope that before it is too late to do anything about it someone of importance, such as yourself, will insist that this uniform be modern, smart, and becoming in both design and colour." She was opposed to the use of khaki and to adapting men's clothing to women's: "Don't you agree with me that since a women's corps is an innovation it is silly to slavishly follow the old idea of the men's army uniform with their throttling collars and ties." After suggesting a uniform based on the style of the day, she concluded, "Please excuse the length of this letter, but no woman likes to look ugly or ridiculous."

The uniform that was eventually issued would not have pleased this correspondent. The uniform for female officers and other ranks of the army consisted of a single-breasted khaki tunic

with two hip pockets, and one breast pocket on the left side. Beech brown epaulettes and beech brown Canada badges on the shoulders are also worn. The gored skirt is slightly flared and worn sixteen inches from the ground. Khaki shirt with beech brown tie, khaki lisle hose and brown oxfords also form part of the uniform. The headdress is a khaki peaked cap, modelled after the French "kepi." The greatcoat is khaki, double-breasted, cavalry pattern, and trimmed with beech brown epaulets.

A raincoat, gloves, overshoes and satchel were also issued. Like members of the other army corps, the women wore uniforms of lightweight material in the summer and serge in the winter. While the CWAC initially used a separate system of rank badges, they switched to the system used by the rest of the army in the spring of 1942, when their auxiliary status changed and they became members of the active militia. As with their counterparts in the RCAF and RCN, army women were given an allowance for the purchase of underclothing. At a conference of senior CWAC officers held in February 1945, the question of personnel wearing the badges of the units with which

they served was raised. After a "full discussion," it was agreed that this was unwise because it would highlight the difference between the servicewomen employed directly by army units and those who remained within the CWAC, resulting in a loss of morale among the latter.

One badge worn by all CWAC members was a constant source of pride. Servicewomen often worked with men who had been conscripted under the *National Resources Mobilization Act* and who were not required to serve overseas. The chief distinction between the two groups was the fact that the CWACs were all volunteers and, as one

Members of the first contingent of CWAC personnel to enter Germany, 12 June 1945. L-R: Sergeant Jane Shaddock, Polly Pollyblank. Private Martin MacPherson is at rear. (NAC, PA 128229)

former member recalls in *Muskeg, Rocks and Rain,* "the most important badge of all had a red 'G.S.' on a black background — meaning the General Service badge — meaning that we were volunteers... So these fellows didn't have a G.S. badge like we did — a fact we never failed to mention to them often."

By January 1942 the army was considering plans to send CWAC personnel overseas. On 14 January a proposal was made to send five hundred women to Great Britain to work in No. 1 Canadian Base Ordnance Workshop, justified by the fact that large numbers of British women were already employed in British army ordnance workshops. The following month Canadian Military Headquarters in London suggested that members of the CWAC replace 150 male soldiers in a static base laundry about to be set up. A growing manpower shortage nullified any concerns about the wisdom of sending women overseas. It was a popular move with the CWAC. One woman who spent the entire war approximately 25 miles from her home recalls, with no small amount of regret, in *Greatcoats and Glamour Boots:* "Overseas duty? Everyone wanted it. I can't think of a single person who wouldn't have given her eye teeth to get over there. That was the whole point!" Another servicewoman, echoing her male counterparts, wanted to "get closer to the action. Of course we didn't know what it was really like. It was just the idea of the excitement and adventure of it all. We weren't even thinking of the dangers." On 6 May 1942, Ottawa approved the dispatch of CWAC personnel to Britain, and Canadian Military Headquarters immediately requested two hundred clerks. The laundry had not yet been built, and although it triggered the deployment of women overseas, in the end it was not laundresses but clerks who first set sail for Britain.

On 18 August 1942 Captain E. Alice Sorby of the CWAC arrived in London to assist in the planning for the first draft. Delays in the provision of suitable accommodation meant that the first detachment, 104 officers and other ranks, did not arrive in Britain until November. There were many subsequent drafts, and servicemen overseas were generally pleased to encounter their female counterparts. So far from Canada, they welcomed the arrival of their country-women as a "link with their homes."

In the early months of 1944 both DND and Canadian Military Headquarters studied the possibility of sending CWAC personnel

Private N. McCosh sorting laundry at Camp Borden, England, 16 March 1945. (NAC, PA 139941)

The CWAC Brass Band, Ottawa, 16 August 1943. (NAC, PA 129066)

Piper Flossie Ross on the deck of German "E" while the CWAC
Pipe Band tours units of the Canadian Army of Occupation
in Wilhelmshaven, Germany, on 4 October 1945.
(NAC, PA 152513)

to the rear areas of operational theatres of war. A positive conclusion was reached and a survey revealed that nearly 1,200 members could be so employed. From very early days, members of the CWAC had also been posted to the United States, including Washington and New York.

Personnel eventually served in Italy, Northwest Europe and the Far East. As they had in Canada and Great Britain, many of these women carried out clerical tasks and adapted to "real army life — under canvas" and vulnerable to nature. As Sergeant Gladys Hurst, who served in France and Belgium, noted in a letter to Alice Sorby: "The boys are grand to us. There is lots of work but we have lots of fun too." Hurst shared a tent with nine other women. She was delighted that the showers sometimes had hot water and made light of waking one morning to find puddles of water by her head and on her stomach after a rainstorm in a leaky tent. Like their predecessors in South Africa and in the First World War, the women improvised to keep warm. Sergeant Hurst found the nights to be the greatest challenge and resorted to wearing extra clothing such as sweaters and socks, although not a balaclava as did one woman in her group.

Over the course of the war more than 21,000 women wore the CWAC uniform, sufficient to release the equivalent of a full division of soldiers for combat duty. Once the first members arrived in the United Kingdom in November 1942, women in the UK who were Canadian by birth, residence or marriage to a Canadian serviceman became eligible to join, and 666 eventually did. As Newfoundland did not have military services open to women, interested Newfoundlanders were free to join the Canadian services, and

some 190 joined the CWAC. Even if these women served "that men may fight," their contribution is nonetheless noteworthy. They received no fewer than 80 honours: four women received an OBE and 15 an MBE, while 42 received a BEM, two a King's Commendation and 16 Mentions-in-Despatches.

Women's Royal Canadian Naval Service, 1942–45

Despite having rejected the idea of employing women in April 1941, by the end of the year the RCN was investigating that very possibility. In January 1942 it asked the British Admiralty to send officers from the Women's Royal Naval Service to assist with the establishment of a Canadian organization. Three officers arrived in May and the federal Cabinet approved the establishment of the WRCNS on 8 May 1942, though official sanction was not received until 31 July. In justifying the creation of the WRCNS, the Minister of National Defence for Naval Services declared that women could take on a range of duties, releasing men for "duties of a heavier nature than they are now performing." The new organization was "to be comprised in and form part of the Naval Forces of Canada and be a component thereof." From the outset, therefore, the WRCNS was an integral part of the RCN, although at first it tended to be treated as an auxiliary.

This situation was a result partly of the influence of the British Wren officers and partly of the lack of familiarity of male naval officers with women in uniform. The order establishing the WRCNS made the Canadian Wren officer the equal of her male counterpart, with "the same power of command exercisable by Officers of the Royal Canadian

A WRCNS signaller wearing bellbottom trousers,
Vancouver, 22 February 1944. (NAC, PA 141002)

Navy of relative rank." The British Women's Royal Naval Service, in contrast, was a distinct and separate organization from the Royal Navy. The various Privy Council orders governing the discharge of women, disability pensions, and the right to transportation at reduced rates for the CWAC and RCAF (WD) were extended to cover the WRCNS.

Candidates for the new service had to be suitably fit and educated as required by the Minister of National Defence for Naval Services. They also had to be: "(a) British subjects of the white race [and] (b) Not less than 18 or more than 45 years of age on the date of attestation; except that specially suitable candidates up to the age of 49 may be entered upon the authority of the Chief of Naval Personnel in each case." The racial

requirement was later dropped but commissions were never granted to women under 21 years of age. Like members of the other organizations, naval servicewomen joined for the duration of hostilities, provided their services were needed, and for duty anywhere they were required.

The first entry class was scheduled for 31 August 1942. A group of 70 women from across Canada assembled. This was the pool from which the navy expected to draw the female officers and petty officers who would play a major role in developing and leading the new organization. Personnel were trained in Galt, Ontario, on the premises of the former Ontario Training School for Girls, a 22-acre property with four dormitories capable of accommodating the administrative officers and between 350 and 400 trainees, six classrooms with typewriters and desks, and a library. Facilities were also available for instruction in cooking.

Providing uniforms for these early recruits proved beyond the means of the RCN. Standing before the fully uniformed British Wren training officers were a motley group of women wearing the wraparound smocks that constituted the only available uniform. Shoes and hats would come later. In the interim, new recruits wore all manner of footwear, from sandals to sensible walking shoes, and hats with the veils and flowers that were the height of fashion in 1942.

WRCNS coders at work in Halifax, June 1944. (NAC, PA 128194)

The uniform they ultimately wore consisted of "a smart navy felt hat, a fitted navy blue double breasted jacket and gored skirt, white shirt, black tie, black shoes and stockings, a navy blue greatcoat and raincoat. The summer uniform is similar, but the suit is in Wren blue." Wren officers wore the blue stripe first worn by the British Wrens as distinction of rank, rather than the gold stripes worn by the male officers. They also wore a tricorn hat with a blue silk badge. Not all Canadian Wrens were happy with their uniform, as is evident from one of their wartime songs, sung to the tune of "Sweet Alice Blue Gown":

WRCNS at switchboard. (NAC, PA 107099)

> *In my sweet little pusser blue gown*
>
> *That I wore that first night into town*
>
> *But what good does it do when you wear pusser blue*
>
> *And your figure looks best in a light frilly dress?*
>
> *Cotton stockings just don't seem to be*
>
> *What a young sailor lad wants to see*
>
> *You're sharp as a thistle, but can't raise a whistle*
>
> *In your sweet little pusser blue gown.*

Canadian women who joined the navy had much to learn, including nautical terminology. They were trained at *stone frigates,* a collection of buildings officially regarded as one of His Majesty's Canadian ships with the appropriate terminology. The kitchen was known as the *galley,* washrooms were *heads* and dormitory rooms were *cabins.* The *quarter-deck* was a wooden platform at the edge of the parade square that all Wrens saluted as they passed, just as sailors saluted the quarter-deck on seagoing vessels. *Liberty Boat* was another naval term that the women of the King's Canadian navy learned quickly. Although not a vessel, it was their passage to freedom during *shore leave,* whether it took the form of a group of Wrens marching from the station or several of them riding off in a bus or truck. Before *going ashore,* the Wrens were inspected from top to toe and could be refused leave for a variety of infractions such as improperly polished shoes, an incorrectly knotted tie or hair that touched the collar. Any infraction would require attention, causing the Wren in question to miss the Liberty Boat and face another inspection before the next *sailing.*

Naval servicewomen replaced men in trades such as stenographers, postal clerks,

Corporal Patricia Johnson, CWAC, working in the kitchen
of Kildare Barracks, Ottawa, 18 April 1944.
(NAC, PA 128252)

Of these, more than five hundred served in Great Britain — at London, Londonderry, Plymouth or HMCS *Niobe* at Greenock — and nearly six hundred in Newfoundland, which at the time was considered an overseas posting. A further 50 or so were stationed in Washington and New York.

For their wartime efforts, 20 servicewomen of the WRCNS received honours: three were awarded the OBE and seven the MBE, while eight received the BEM and two a King's Commendation.

stewards, coders, cooks, pay writers, motor transport drivers, teletype operators and laundry workers. Provision was made at the outset for the opening of additional trades to women as the need arose. However, for trades that had a direct civilian application, such as stenographers and cooks, only experienced personnel were recruited. Before the end of the war, necessity dictated the introduction of training in a variety of trades, for, as the Canadian Wren Song stated, the women had to "Carry on! Carry on! Sailor boys must sail!"

The first group to be posted to the UK arrived late in 1943, but until January 1945 it was found necessary to keep "borrowing" British Wrens for the various RCN shore establishments and commands in Britain. The navy continued to recruit women until February 1945 and the peak strength achieved was almost six thousand all ranks.

Canadian Servicewomen in the War: Recruiting, Discipline and Daily Life

For the most part, servicewomen were called upon to perform tasks that, in the social ethos of the time, were seen as suitable for their gender. On one occasion, for example, the army and air force put out an urgent call for "Canadian women who have felt the desire to slap down Hitler with a skillet" to join up as military cooks. Women did not need to be culinary experts or dietitians. They simply had to possess "elementary knowledge and liking" for the task. The armed forces called upon women to serve "so that men may fight," and many servicewomen did believe that by joining up they would be releasing men for service, but the results were not always satisfying. As one French-Canadian woman recalls in *Greatcoats and Glamour Boots*: "...when I'd read the

66 Women War Artists

by Martine Turenne

IT WAS NOT UNTIL LATE IN THE SECOND WORLD WAR that the first few Canadian women war artists appeared on the scene, and even then, none of them ever visited the front, or even travelled to Europe or Asia, during the hostilities. Nonetheless, each of them made, in her own way, a distinct contribution to the body of 13,000 works – paintings, watercolours, drawings, prints and sculptures – that make up the Canadian War Museum collection.

The first program designed to present a specifically Canadian vision of the great military events of the time was put in place in 1916, about halfway through the First World War, mainly through the efforts of Lord Beaverbrook, a Canadian millionaire living in London. Beaverbrook commissioned photographers and painters to portray various aspects of the war as experienced by Canadians. The resulting creations dealt with subjects such as daily life in the barracks, trench warfare, the great battles, the horrors of war and the euphoria of the Armistice celebrations.

Among the most notable of the artists who went to Europe to take part in the program were A.Y. Jackson, Frederick Varley, Arthur Lismer and Franz Johnston all of them future members of the famous Group of Seven.

Beaverbrook's original plan was to erect a memorial art gallery to house the thousand pieces created by Canadian war artists during the First World War. The undertaking was never completed, however, and the paintings – some as large as four-by-six metres – remained more or less out of the public view for many years.

Lord Beaverbrook's war art program did not resume when Canada joined the Allied forces at the outbreak of the Second World War. It was, in fact, 1943 before a full-fledged Canadian war art program finally came into being, largely due to the drive and energy of two highly persuasive men, Vincent Massey, the Canadian High Commissioner in London, and Harry McCurry, Director of the National Gallery. Despite numerous obstacles, the two men did eventually manage to get the project officially approved, and a nationwide contest was launched to determine who would take part. Artists such as Alex Colville, Charles Comfort, Henry Lamb and Bruno Bobak were among those chosen to be the first to cross the Atlantic as participants in the program. In all, about artists contributed a total of some 5,000 works to the collection, works that were, in general, smaller, more stylized and bolder than their more traditional Great War predecessors.

Half a dozen women participated in the collective effort. They included Paraskeva Clark, Lilias Newton and Pegi Nicol MacLeod. But it was Molly Lamb, a 23-year-old officer, who became the only one to actually wear a uniform. She visited the European battle areas (albeit only after the close of hostilities) and was granted the official title of war artist.

The war as seen
by Molly Lamb Bobak

In June 1945, Molly Lamb landed in newly liberated Europe with her brushes, a few canvases and the mission of capturing on those canvases both the climate of devastation and the essence of the day-to-day life of Canada's women soldiers. It was an experience that would change her life forever. "I didn't suffer," she says, somewhat apologetically, "but so many people did. By the time I arrived, the war was over."

Today, at seventy-eight years of age, Molly Lamb Bobak has lost nothing of the vivacity, humour and zest for life typical of Lamb as a young new recruit in the Canadian Women's Army Corps in 1942.

Frederick Varley's vivid images of the horrors of another war that had bathed Europe in blood twenty-five years earlier, and an innate sense of duty, drove her to join the struggle against Hitler.

Molly Lamb Bobak has never stopped painting. When I visited her at her home in Fredericton one cold, grey morning in early May, she raced down the stairs from her third-floor studio, where, just as every other morning, she had been painting. She wore jeans, a little sweater and a pale smock; her hands were covered in paint, and her greeting of "Hi" was delivered with a big smile, her laughter ready just below the surface. These days, she paints seascapes: people on the beach looking towards the ocean, little dabs of colour in the immense

grey and blue. Serious eye problems make it difficult for her to paint, "but I keep going. It's what I've done all my life."

She offered me a glass of sherry, and we sat down at the kitchen table in her lovely, rustic house on a quiet street near the Saint John River. She was born near the Pacific, but for the past forty years she has lived in the Maritimes with her husband, the painter Bruno Bobak. In 1960 he was named resident artist at the Art Centre of the University of New Brunswick and soon afterwards became the Centre's director, occupying the post until his retirement.

Molly Lamb grew up on the wild, grandiose beaches of Burnaby Lake in a Vancouver suburb, living "a happy childhood," with plenty of space and freedom. Her parents were an atypical, nonconformist couple who never married. Her father, H. Mortimer Lamb, who came to Canada from England in 1885, was a critic, an art collector and a devotee of a new form of visual expression, photography. He was a friend to artists and an early supporter of the Group of Seven, some of whose members he got to know while he was president of the Canadian Mining Association in Montreal. Alex Jackson and Frederick Varley became frequent visitors to his west coast home.

In those days Vancouver was only a small town, but it was home to an art school that did justice to its name, Emily Carr College, where Montrealer Charles Scott was director. Molly Lamb enrolled in the school in 1938, at the age of sixteen, happy and relieved at quitting high school, which had bored her half to death. At the college, she was introduced to the visual arts by Jack Shadbolt, a professor whom she still considers one of her mentors. One of his works hangs in a room on the second floor of her house. "I didn't paint like him, but what I got from him was his passion for painting."

Having completed her studies, she joined the army at twenty years of age, in November 1942. I ask her what attraction barracks and a uniform held for a young artist. "It was quite natural; I didn't think about it very much," she replies. "I was looking for adventure, a change of scenery, I believe. And we all hated Hitler!"

She arrived at the barracks in Vancouver full of enthusiasm and very naïve. Transferred to Camp Vermilion in Alberta soon afterwards, she experienced extreme cold for the first time; it was thirty-three below on the Canadian prairies in the early winter, and she had neither hat nor gloves! Above all, what she discovered in

Molly Lamb Bobak, 1922–
Roman Catholic Church Parade, Ottawa
Oil on canvas, 76.3 cm x 56 cm

CWM - 12080

the barracks was a world of women. "Contrary to what one might think, there were many women in the army at the time," she explains. In fact, there were about 45,000 women enlisted in the Canadian Armed Forces, doing administrative tasks or working in the obscurity of the kitchens or the laundry.

After Alberta, she crisscrossed the country: Winnipeg, Ottawa, Toronto, Halifax and Montreal, which she describes in her diary as "the most exciting city in the world," with its cathedrals, traditions and restaurants in which she ordered "some Bordeaux *très rouge*." She hung out with young women from all over the country: farm women, city women, intellectuals, workers, women from every social class, all made equal by wearing the same uniform, living the same barracks life and taking the same long train trips. "Is that what we had in common?" Molly Lamb wonders. All the women, she noted in her diary, were basically the same, whatever their origin.

Private Lamb, happy and full of life, threw herself into her favourite pastime, drawing. That's how an original work, *W1100278 – the Diary of a C.W.A.C.*, came into being, full of humour and spirit, a prelude to the canvases she would eventually paint when she was officially designated as a war artist. Kept between November 1942 and June 1945, the diary contains 147 folios and over forty-eight sketches and paintings, produced in charcoal, ink, pencil and watercolour. It has been conserved since 1989 in the collection of the National Archives of Canada. Everywhere she went, Molly Lamb carried the diary in a portfolio she had made herself. Conceived and edited like a conventional diary, it describes daily events with much charm, wit and skill, notes Carolyn Gossage, who published it in 1992.[1] In the diary, Molly Lamb recalls anecdotes and reflections. "I had a lot of time on my hands," says Lamb Bobak. "Too much! Sometimes I got a little bored. So I drew; I painted."

W1100278 – the Diary of a C.W.A.C. is "humbly dedicated to A.Y. Jackson," the friend and painter whom she met when she was on leave in Toronto. "Uncle Alex," as she called him, became her mentor, introducing her to Charles Comfort, who had visited Canadian troops overseas on several occasions. She dreamed of emulating him, she wrote in her diary, even if she didn't believe she ever would.

Meanwhile, Alex Jackson sent a letter to Harry McCurry, Director of the National Gallery, to tell him about his discovery: there was a young woman in the Canadian Army who was portraying women's life in the barracks as only a woman could. "Very real stuff" was the way he described her drawings. As it happened, McCurry had just received funding to resume the war artist program. A national contest was announced, and Jackson urged his protégé to enter it.

Molly Lamb finished second in the contest, just behind Bruno Bobak, who would become her husband a few years later. She showed me the prize-winning work, *Pay Parade*, hanging on the wall on the second floor of her house; it depicts a line of women soldiers waiting for their pay outside the barracks in Hamilton, just before nightfall in October 1943.

Meanwhile, a few excerpts from her diary were published in the magazine *New World*. For the first time in her life, she saw her drawings in print. It was a shock…and a very exciting moment, she wrote.

To become a war artist officially, Molly Lamb trained as an officer in Sainte-Anne-de-Bellevue, Quebec. Training was a formality, she says, but returning to Montreal and discovering Quebec was very gratifying: "For the first time, I was faced with a real cultural difference. It would come in handy in Europe and for the rest of my life."

Though Molly Lamb was the only woman in uniform who had the title of war artist, she wasn't the only one to paint scenes of daily life in the army. Other "civilians" covered the barracks: Paraskeva Clark, Lilias Newton and especially Pegi Nicol MacLeod. By 1943, MacLeod, a Toronto artist who would die of cancer four years after the war ended, had already earned a reputation among military painters. "Everyone talked about her and I'd seen a few of her canvases," recalls Molly Lamb Bobak. "One day when I was at the National Gallery in Ottawa, I spotted a woman with a very short haircut. It was Pegi. I rushed over to her, as enthusiastic as ever, and I told her, 'You're a wonderful artist!' She laughed. She was very friendly, a true artist."

Molly showed me Pegi Nicol MacLeod's self-portrait hanging in the second-floor hallway next to works by A.Y. Jackson, Jeff MacDonald and Arthur Lismer. Which of these artists had the biggest influence on her when she decided to portray military life? The Group of Seven, she says, and…Cézanne. "I love the

---

1. GOSSAGE, Carolyn, *Double Duty*, Toronto: Dundurn Press, 1992.

Molly Lamb Bobak, 1922–
Private Roy, CWAC
Oil on masonite, 76.3 cm x 60.7 cm

CWM - 12082

Molly Lamb Bobak, 1922–
Baseball Game in Hyde Park, London
Watercolour, ink, charcoal and carbon pencil on paper, 38.2 cm x 55.9 cm

CWM - 12005

structure, the construction of his paintings, the way he understands things. It makes me want to cry when I see one of his paintings." Among the war artists, she admires James William Morris, who was in the trenches in 1914–18 ("...his personal touch, his vision").

Molly Lamb, now Lieutenant Lamb, travelled across the country from barracks to barracks, recording daily life. Her paintings included the famous portrait *Private Roy*, done in 1944 and named for its subject, a black woman stationed in Halifax, shown standing behind a counter in a canteen. "I tried to look her up," says Molly Lamb Bobak, "and others, too, but in vain. It's odd, isn't it? She just vanished into thin air."

Molly Lamb Bobak's paintings had to reflect reality, but, like all the artists of the time, she played with the forms, deconstructed them, transformed them. The works of the Second World War were less formal than those of the First, but the subject was what counted, she says. I ask her if the fact that her one trip to Europe occurred only after the war's end was the Army's way of protecting her from the horrors of war and the fighting. She doesn't believe it for a moment. "I became a war artist too late," she says. "I think it was just a combination of circumstances, and not because I was a woman."

The conversation turns to the slippery subject of women in the army. We talk about the scandals that have come to light in recent years, carrying allegations of everything from paternalism to harassment, assault and rape. Molly Lamb Bobak is visibly annoyed by the fuss. "I was never harassed," she insists in no uncertain terms. "There's so much exaggeration about all that. Everyone's complaining; everyone's a victim." It was wartime; the guys teased the girls, had a good laugh with them. Sure, says Molly Lamb Bobak, in the army there were brutal generals, stupid recruits. "Once I kicked a soldier in the stomach. It wasn't serious, and I didn't make a big thing about it! In those days, we accepted things as they were."

In June 1945 she boarded the *Île de France*, which sailed from Halifax to Glasgow. The troops she saw in London were haggard, exhausted, demoralized. "The soldiers were eager to return home," she says. "Some of them had been in Europe for four or five years. They had had enough." Her mission remained the same: to record on canvas the daily life of women soldiers.

The Europe she encountered was morose, sad, devastated. For four months she visited troops stationed in Belgium, Holland and Germany. She stopped over a few times in Paris, which was "so sad," then went to the concentration camp at Bergen-Belsen. Molly Lamb Bobak has never gotten over the heaps of human bones, the huge common graves. "It was horrible." But, she insists, it was another Canadian war artist, Aba Bayefsky, who gave the most deeply disturbing testimony, in a dozen paintings made after a visit to Bergen-Belsen a few months earlier.

Her method was to make quick sketches onsite and later rework them in a London studio. You can find everything in her art: the life of young women in the barracks, daily tasks, long marches in the countryside, Sunday morning Mass, and leisure time activities too, as shown, for example, in the painting of an evening in a London pub, or her depiction of a baseball game in Hyde Park. And of course there are the victory celebrations in London in August 1945.

However, she insists, she never saw the horrors of war, the fighting, and the front. "I was spared all that. I didn't suffer; I wasn't traumatized. I didn't die like the millions of people who never returned home." At the time, she says, people were just beginning to count the victims. The scope of the disaster was a distant rumour, much like the magnitude of what went on in the concentration camps.

She returned to Canada in 1946. She had changed without really being aware of it. What happened during the war, she says, was only a digression in her life, "a time out of time," in Charles Comfort's apt words. But what followed "was another story." First, marriage, then, soon afterwards, a son named Alex in honour of A.Y. Jackson. And, finally, a career as an artist, which got off to a spectacular start because of the renown she had gained during the war.

The works she and her colleagues painted have been more or less forgotten; they are virtually unknown to the public. "It's a pity," she says. "Sure, war photography, which is more instantaneous, immediate, malleable, has had a more significant impact. Painting...is more meditative. But both artistic expressions have their place when you report reality. Especially the reality of war."

Martine Turenne is a journalist for *L'Actualité* magazine.

Molly Lamb Bobak, 1922–
Gas Drill
Oil on canvas, 68.8 cm x 86.8 cm

CWM - 12059

Pegi Nicol MacLeod, 1904–49
Untitled
Oil on panel, 73.2 cm x 65.4 cm

CWM - 14231

Molly Lamb Bobak, 1922–
CWAC's Officer Cadets and N.C.O.'s Waiting
for the Montreal Train
Oil on masonite, 60.6 cm x 76.1 cm

CWM - 12035

Paraskeva Clark, 1898–1986
Parachute Riggers
Oil on canvas, 101.8 cm x 81.4 cm

CWM - 14086

Molly Lamb Bobak, 1922–
CWAC's Sorting Mail
Oil on canvas, 61 cm x 76.3 cm

CWM - 12051

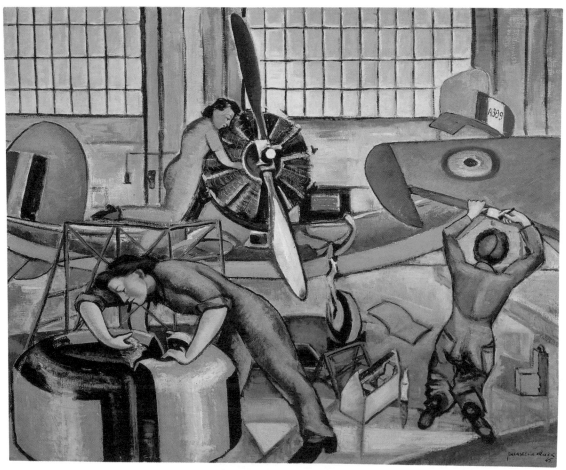

Paraskeva Clark, 1898–1986
Maintenance Jobs in the Hangar
Oil on canvas, 81.5 cm x 101.9 cm

CWM - 14085

Molly Lamb Bobak, 1922–
The Bathhouse
Watercolour on paper, 30.4 cm x 28.9 cm

CWM - 12012

Molly Lamb Bobak, 1922–
CWAC Barracks
Oil on canvas, 76.2 x 101.5 cm

CWM - 12019

Molly Lamb Bobak, 1922–
Boat Drill, Emergency Stations
Oil on canvas, 61 cm x 71 cm

CWM - 12013

casualty lists in the papers, I'd say to myself, it's true, I am doing something to help, but the boy I've relieved for overseas duty might very well end up getting himself killed. So my sentiments were mixed. It was hard to know what was right."

The Governor-General, the Earl of Athlone, added his voice to the call for women to enlist. In "Tribute to the Canadian Women's Army Corps," which appeared in the recruiting booklet *CWAC Digest: Facts About the CWAC,* he spoke of the interesting life that awaited them and of "the satisfaction of knowing that they are indeed nobly serving their country in the time of its greatest crisis." In a novel twist on the notion that the women would be required to leave their traditional sphere, the Governor-General called upon them to don uniforms "not in order to replace men in men's jobs, but to take from men jobs which, in time of war, are much more suitable to women."

There was a multitude of motivations for women to join the armed forces — some practical and others reflecting a romanticized view. Patriotism was often mentioned, although usually as a secondary factor. Confesses an unnamed airwoman in *Women in Khaki:* "Though I suppose I was as loyal and patriotic as most Canadian girls, I joined because I thought life in the service would improve me as a person." A number of women saw military service as an opportunity for a steady job or free training. Recruiting materials certainly did emphasize the wide range of trades open to women and the training available to them. Unfortunately, however, the reality was that the vast majority of servicewomen were employed in such traditionally feminine occupations as clerks,

stenographers, cooks and food-service providers.

For some women, the appeal of joining up was the promise of escape from their job or the reality of everyday life. Leading Airwoman Sarah E. Johnson, a young woman from New Brunswick, remembers in *To Spread Their Wings* that she was "not alone in finding the Air Force a marvellous release

Members of the CWAC disembark in England, 1942. (CFPU, PL 14642)

from poverty, drudgery and no hope of getting out of it." The Depression had shaped the lives of Canadians for so long that the Second World War offered hope of relief. There were also those daughters who were seeking a way out of the family home; for these women, the desire to serve their country was, just as it was for Canadian men, enough to get them to a recruiting centre. In many other instances it was simply a case of the tradition of public service being extended to encompass military service. An analysis of the applications of the first women to join the air force revealed that 41 per cent had connections with the Red Cross, 23 per cent with voluntary war services and 15 per cent with the Girl Guides.

The loss of a loved one in the war — a husband, sweetheart or brother — was

Canadian servicewomen travelling to Newfoundland, an "overseas" posting, circa 1942. (CFPU, PL 11316)

sometimes the impetus. On a lighter note, though, some women confessed to enlisting in order to be closer to their husbands or boyfriends. How often the vagaries of the posting system brought them together is unknown. One woman reports in *Six War Years* that she enlisted because "the man I was engaged to was in it and overseas and I, dumb that I was, thought it would be the best way to get over to him." When she was eventually posted to Great Britain she discovered her love had already married a British woman. Some women joined because they thought they owed it to their sons in uniform, while some daughters of men who had fought in the First World War saw enlisting as natural or even "necessary." Other women were drawn to the military in general or to one of the services by the uniforms, while still others were attracted by the promise of travel and adventure. Endorsements by current members drew some women to enlist, and then there were groups of friends who decided to join up together. Some — their confidence bolstered by the presence of their friends — were rudely awakened when, after signing up, they learned they were the only member of the group considered suitable.

RCAF recruitment literature took on the theme "that men may fly." "When a girl joins the Women's Division of the RCAF," declared one brochure, "She releases a man to fly and fight; She does a war job of prime importance to Canada, AND she also takes training that will be valuable to her for the rest of her life." (It was made clear that the training was a bargain: if provided through civilian schools, it would have been

Bob Hope Show on tour, Bremen, Germany, 24 July 1945: L-R: Nursing Sister Lilian Tweedy, comedian Bob Hope, Nursing Sister Lilian Owens, Jerry Colonna of the US Army, Nursing Sister Margaret Perley. (NAC, PA 137475)

expensive.) Along with the free medical care, the physical training would keep the servicewoman in good health, and she could expect to meet girls who shared her sense of patriotism and "whose hearts, like hers, beat to the rhythm of the planes." The campaign "Mon père voudrait-il que je m'enrôle?" (Would my dad want me to join?) informed Canadians of the benefits of serving with the RCAF (WD): food prepared under the supervision of dietitians, professional medical and dental services, working hours similar to those of civilians, and leisure hours filled with sports, amusements and relaxation. A number of the men in air force blue had the pleasure of seeing their daughters join the RCAF (WD).

With the reputation of servicewomen seen as key to recruitment in all three organizations, there was much concern about scandal and immorality. Early in 1943, when recruitment campaigns were crucial to maintaining the supply of women, the CWAC faced a drop in enlistment. In order to find the cause and a solution, it hired a polling firm to conduct a public opinion survey. The results showed that the Canadian public did not believe women should be joining the military and many thought that those who did join were immoral. One member of the military described the public hostility towards army servicewomen: "If people saw a boy and a girl walking hand-in-hand down by the Rideau Canal together they'd say, 'Oh, look at that nice young couple.' But if the girl was in Army uniform, they'd say, 'Oh, look at that cheap CWAC'." CWACs and other servicewomen had little patience for those who disgraced the uniform and wanted them discharged at

Students at HMCS *St. Hyacinthe* Signal School, St. Hyacinthe, Quebec, September 1944. (NAC, PA 150940)

once. All three services worked hard at focusing public attention on the valuable contribution made by their women personnel and sought to screen out "undesirable" applicants. Meanwhile, the services had to rely on the example of their female personnel, whose behaviour was for the most part beyond reproach.

One of the most pressing problems, and one of particular concern because of the message it conveyed to potential recruits and their families, was pregnancy among single women, the highest rate of which was found in servicewomen aged 19 to 24. The CWAC consultant to the Director-General of Medical Services identified "insufficient recreational facilities in some localities coupled with drinking in unsupervised places [as] the greatest contributing factors" to unplanned

CWAC softball champs at Argyll Barracks, circa 1944. (NAC, PA 129064)

Lieutenant-Colonel Alice Sorby, Deputy Director of CWAC Overseas, and Lieutenant-Colonel Isobel Cronyn, Deputy Director of CWAC, at NDHQ, London, England, 13 February 1945. (NAC, PA 129091)

pregnancy. The responsibility for rectifying these situations, she argued, rested with the whole army, not just the CWAC.

Once the women were recruited, there was the issue of training them. With the exception of the RCAMC Nursing Service, the organizations in which women served had come into being from nothing, so senior staff in all three services had to ponder the problem of training female recruits. The usual questions of *who, what, where, when* and *why* had to be addressed, and one particular dilemma was whether women should be instructed by male or female personnel. Military decision-makers were advised by way of a staff memorandum that "It is felt that women will take more kindly to instruction in military subjects from an experienced male officer or soldier than they will from one of their own...as they are quick to realize that the latter personnel can have only a very limited background." For the women

trainees, the *why* was often all too clear — the military wanted to determine which of them would prove suitable for the armed forces. Basic training often proved difficult for their male counterparts as well — regulations were strict and the hours were completely different from those in civilian life. Also, physical activity in the military was more rigorous than most women were accustomed to, and those who could not meet the standards were weeded out.

Conversely, the wearing of a uniform proved to be a popular aspect of military life. During the Great Depression many women had been preoccupied with finding a way to clothe themselves, and in the service they received not only a complete uniform but also an allowance for underclothing and upkeep. In *To Spread Their Wings*, Sara Johnson recalls her sense of pride in her uniform and her satisfaction at the knowledge that she "would never have to worry about what to wear" and "would always be properly dressed for every occasion." When it came to the matter of the uniform itself, of course, women were no different from men — rarely would a new recruit be issued one that fitted to the satisfaction of the wearer and his or her officer. Neither did the uniform always please the fashion-conscious, but the presence of their badge of service and the pride it instilled was most important. The exclusivity of a military uniform pleased the servicewoman. It indicated that she belonged to an institution dedicated to a cause: male members of the armed forces were recognized for their achievements on the battlefield, at sea and in the air, and servicewomen shared pride in their accomplishments.

With minor adjustments for women, discipline in Canada's armed forces was the same for the two sexes. Punishment could seem extremely harsh to a woman new to military life. A "drumming out parade" for one miscreant stuck in the memory of a Wren who had witnessed it. She recounts the experience in *Greatcoats and Glamour Boots:* "...taking all the buttons off her uniform and all her badges, and the whole public humiliation of it all, being marched off, stripped of everything, including your dignity. But that was the idea, I guess, to make it so dramatic that it would serve as a deterrent to the others."

The role of officer in a small women's organization could be a difficult one. For example, on air force stations an officer with the WDs might bend the rules and befriend the same airwomen she would later have to discipline. This illustrates why officers were not encouraged to fraternize with enlisted personnel. Though many officers had begun their service careers as enlisted personnel, relationships formed in the early days became inappropriate once an officer's insignia was sewn on the uniform. Promotion could also mean leaving the camaraderie of an all-women's mess for an integrated mess, perhaps as the only woman.

The military has a long tradition of providing recreational activities, and the wartime women's organizations were no exception. Organized sports such as softball, badminton, tennis, hockey and swimming were all offered where facilities permitted, while picnics, hiking, skiing and table tennis were among the less strenuous pursuits. Concerts, plays

and choral presentations were featured on stations and bases where the talent could be found. Relaxing in the canteen was always popular, as were military-sponsored dances. On isolated stations, where women were greatly outnumbered by men, they took precautions to avoid trouble, often travelling in groups or pairs when off duty. Memories are not always without sarcasm, judging by an account in *Greatcoats and Glamour Boots:* "Most men were truly in love with only you (and the balance of your platoon)." As recalled in *Petticoat Warfare,* women also encountered problems in adapting to a totally new environment: "What a merry-go-round

Members of the CWAC on tennis court in Ottawa, 30 June 1944. (NAC, PA 139932)

for the naive eighteen-year-olds who came straight from the prairies, and in some cases isolated from their nearest neighbour by as much as fifty miles. Without the advantage of specific sex education at home, their knowledge of life was pitifully scarce."

Woman modelling a lime-green spun-rayon dress suggested for purchase as part of the CWAC discharge clothing allowance of $100, at Glebe Collegiate, Ottawa, 23 October 1945. (NAC, PA 128258)

Servicewomen were always keenly aware that there was a war on. Sarah Johnson remembers in *To Spread Their Wings,* with a tinge of guilt, that "it used to gnaw at my conscience that I was having such a good time because there was a war on — [my life in the armed forces] would never have happened otherwise — and because there was a war on, other people were dying and suffering horrors beyond my imagining... It seemed a terrible price to pay for my happiness." Christmas could bring together a group of brothers and sisters all in uniform. Johnson recalls that "it was a nice change to be on a more equal footing with my brother." She tried to convince her sister to join as well, believing that she would benefit from the experience, but her brother-in-law argued successfully against the idea. A peaceful Christmas Day spent in the safety of a Canadian military base illustrated the difference between serving overseas and serving at home. Those in Canada, for the festive season at least, were grateful they were far from the guns and bombs.

Canadian Servicewomen, 1939–45: A Successful Experiment

When all was said and done, the enlistment of women during the Second World War was an impressive achievement. Of the nearly 50,000 servicewomen who volunteered to serve their country, 71 gave their lives. Despite the near-universal desire for overseas service, only one in nine members of the three women's organizations served outside Canada, although nursing officers had a higher rate of overseas service than others. The experiment of raising women's organizations had proved entirely successful. In 1939 few would have conceived of women serving in the armed forces in any occupation but nursing. In 1945, Commander William Strange, Director of Naval Information,

A member of the CWAC weds a member of the Navy at Kildare Barracks,
Ottawa, 24 April 1945. (NAC, PA 139928)

spoke about the WRCNS, but his statement applied equally to all three women's organizations:

[I]t seems almost impossible that there should be a Navy without them. So thoroughly did they become part of the Navy during the *days of great emergency, that now that the emergency has passed it is going to be hard for many who have remained to realize that they were, in actual fact, an emergency force.*

Disbandment was a foregone conclusion.

Captain Elizabeth Pense, RCAMC, being invested with the Royal Red Cross medal by Major-General M.M.A.R. West, Korea, 30 May 1952. (NAC, PA 128041)

Chapter III

A TIME OF UNCERTAINTY: 1945–65

The Service has been a man's world for centuries and it is only yesterday in history that women have been granted the privilege of serving in the Navy.
— *Handbook for WREN Officers,* 1962

Demobilization, 1945–46, and the End of the Women's Organizations

Long before the final defeat of the Axis powers, the repatriation of personnel serving overseas and the demobilization of those members who had enlisted "for the duration" were the subject of much discussion by military staff. The government, with the agreement of the three services, established a plan for civilian departments to administer all matters relating to the rehabilitation of wartime personnel, including discharge procedures, dispersal of bonuses and gratuities, and dissemination of information.

The end of hostilities did not signal the immediate return of women to civilian life. There were, after all, hundreds of thousands of men overseas who had been in uniform much longer, and getting them home first

Discharge of last member of the RCAF (WD), 1 March 1947. (CFPU, PL 117212)

was official policy. The government put in place a system based on the principle of "first in, first out," whereby the longest serving were to be the first to return, with those wounded or taken prisoner of war receiving the highest priority for repatriation. The need to provide personnel for the occupation of Germany and for the overall administration of the three services influenced the implementation of the plan. Thus members of the

women's organizations overseas settled down to wait, as did many servicewomen in Canada, while long-service male personnel were demobilized, along with those deemed "surplus to requirements."

Demobilization — and the paperwork that inevitably accompanies it — required administration, a field in which women service personnel had proved themselves. They also took on new jobs, both in Canada and overseas, as the men who had been doing them left military service. There were exceptions. Married women were demobilized from the Royal Canadian Air Force (Women's Division) beginning in November 1944, although widows were classified as single and kept on strength, while married women whose husbands were prisoners of war and those in special circumstances could apply to remain in the service.

In March 1945 there were 11,790 people serving with the WD, but by the end of August 1945 only 9,942 airwomen were still in uniform and in March 1946 the figure was a little over three thousand. Between March 1945 and March 1946 the number of WDs serving overseas dropped from 1,360 to 480. Some personnel ready for demobilization were sought for transfer to the Canadian Women's Army Corps (CWAC), which saw a long-term need for female service members. The remaining women in the WD were demobilized by March 1947.

A similar process occurred in the CWAC. By the end of August 1945, 8,216 personnel had left the organization. Of the remaining force of 13,304 women, 4,353 were demobilized by the end of December 1945 and the final 9,051 during the first eight months of 1946. On 15 August 1946, Major Maria A. Morrisson and Private Beatrice O. Charles, the last servicewomen to return from overseas, arrived in Halifax, and before the month was out the CWACs remaining in Washington were back in Canada.

The Women's Royal Canadian Naval Service (WRCNS) was also governed by the "first in, first out" policy, but a number of exceptions were made. Personnel who were married to men who had been discharged prior to September 1945 were entitled to demobilization regardless of the length of their service, but if a Wren's husband was still in the military she was treated according to the established system. Of the 6,781 women who had joined up, some 1,600 had already left the service by the end of August 1945. Between September and December 1945 a further 1,802 returned to civilian life, and by the end of 1946 the remaining 3,357 had been demobilized.

Discussion of the dissolution of the women's organizations cannot pass without some mention of the attempts to prevent it. Senior staff in all three services had recommended that a small cadre of women be retained as a nucleus on which to build in the event of another war. However, although the wartime contribution of servicewomen was seen as valuable, the government was eager to demobilize as many people as possible. There were also continuing and widespread doubts about the suitability of military life for women. Even Captain (Naval) Adelaide H.G. Sinclair, Director WRCNS, commented in 1946 on the wisdom of retaining women in the postwar navy. The usefulness of such a small number, she said, did not justify the staff required to train them. Sinclair also contended that "communal uniformed life does not appeal to most women" and that in time of peace they would not submit to the necessary training and discipline. She recommended that women eager to stay in the navy be encouraged to seek civilian employment, thus saving the Royal Canadian Navy (RCN) the inconvenience of keeping them in the permanent force. The army had no more success with the CWAC, but army staff at least made the provision of listing all ex-members who wished it in the supplementary reserve. Nor did the air force succeed with its "RCAF (Women's Division) Plan for Organization and Suggestions Concerning Employment," dated October 1946. This proposal to rebuild the division met with firm refusal.

By contrast, the end of the war had little impact on the work of the nurses. Thousands of servicemen still required care, but as the three services gradually closed their overseas medical establishments they released nurses from service. Some returned to civilian hospitals or resumed their studies, but the majority continued to nurse their wartime patients, now relocated to veterans' hospitals set up across Canada. These women were responding to a call by Matron-in-Chief Agnes Macleod on behalf of the Department of Veterans' Affairs (DVA) to "build up a service of which Canada can be proud" to "repay in small measure the men who risked all, and who deserve the services of the best medical service possible." The service hospitals in Montreal, Winnipeg, Calgary and Vancouver were integrated with the DVA hospitals in these cities. This arrangement permitted advanced diagnostic and treatment facilities and extended the training and experience of military medical staff.

Postwar organization of the regular force component of the three services provided for a much reduced nursing establishment — 30 positions each in the army and the RCAF and 20 in the RCN. Entry was through the reserve force, since, in 1947, nurses in the reserve were permitted to apply for regular commissions of limited duration — varying between three and seven years — in order to guarantee a steady flow of personnel.

After initial postwar downsizing, the nursing service of the RCAF steadily grew as women were posted to outlying stations and to larger air stations such as Trenton and Rockcliffe. From time to time a nurse might be called on to be part of a "mercy flight" bringing a particularly ill patient to a station hospital. However, although a select group of nurses had been trained in air evacuation in 1943, it would be five years before another flight nurse qualified. Thereafter, yearly courses were held to train nurses in aeromedical work.

At base and station military hospitals, nurses cared for military patients, their dependents and, on occasion, civilian employees. If the base was isolated, their job frequently included the role of public health nurse to the community at large. Isolated posts had their hazards, as Major Noreen Cambon recounts in *The Military Nurses of Canada*. Polar bears would often amble into Fort Churchill, Manitoba, where she was stationed, and while they were "beautiful beasts who travel very quickly" they were "not friendly to people." Cambon recounts experiencing "chills" when she realized one of these enormous furry visitors had spotted her.

Re-establishment of the Women's Organizations, 1949–55

At the end of the Second World War, as at the end of the Great War, Canadians entertained the hope that cooperation would replace conflict as a means of resolving international disputes. The massive demobilization that took place in 1945–46 was not unique to Canada; proportionately, the United States reduced its military forces even more rapidly, and the other allied nations followed suit. In hindsight, it was optimistic and perhaps politically expedient to expect that the postwar world would be so safe that large armed forces would be unnecessary, but such thinking was the reality of the day.

With the Communist coup in Czechoslovakia in February 1948 and the Berlin blockade a month later, Canada and her former allies were forced to acknowledge the existence of a "cold war." While most allied powers had reduced their military force, the Soviet Union had maintained a powerful force in service that continued to occupy Eastern European nations, keeping Communist governments in power. Increasing tensions among the former allies led to the gradual re-armament of the Western powers, including Canada. It soon became apparent that if recruiting targets were to be met, the women's service organizations would have to be re-established.

In late 1950, at the outset of the Korean War, the federal Cabinet authorized the recruitment of women into the regular force to supplement available manpower. The government's intention was to use women's military organizations not to replace female civil servants but to supplement their strength. Early in 1951 the Cabinet Defence Committee was informed that women were urgently needed by all three services. Pressing the point further, a memorandum acknowledged that women would be required in any future war and that the "recruitment of women in peace time can fill vacancies for which it is difficult to recruit men, and at the same time build up reserve cadres which would ease mobilization problems."

The government set limitations. The number of women recruits had to be accommodated within the legislated total establishments, or maximum number allowed, of each service and there were to be no special units for women. No servicewomen were to be employed at the service headquarters in Ottawa, as had been the case with the women's organizations in the Second World War. Finally, women were not to replace civilian workers.

Recruitment literature for the postwar women's organizations emphasized the "feminine" and "stylish" qualities of the uniforms, an unnamed fashion expert declaring them "more feminine and smarter

than the wartime outfit." Gushed a 1954 recruiting circular for the WRCNS:

Although a Wren must be intelligent and well-trained to take her place in the modern Navy, the Service has not forgotten that she is a woman and wants to look attractive. Wren uniforms were designed for compliments. Wartime Wrens were delighted with their uniforms, but today's Wrens look even smarter. The tailoring of the uniforms is better, nylon stockings have been added, and so has a trim two-tone outfit for summer.

A woman enlists as nurse in the RCAF, 10 July 1961. (CFPU, PL 72364)

Perhaps one of the more positive aspects of the uniform policy in the postwar organizations was that women did not have to wear them off duty, whereas wartime regulations specified that the uniform was to be worn except on leaves of more than 48 hours. Clearly the RCAF recruiters thought this was a change worth trumpeting: "During off-duty

Para-rescue nurse Marian Neiley, May 1955.
(CFPU, PL 130186)

hours and while on leave, airwomen enjoy the time-honoured feminine privilege of dressing as they please in civilian clothes."

Servicewomen were particularly useful in locations where civilian labour was scarce. While the army and navy sought to enlist women into their reserve components only, the air force identified a need in both its regular and reserve units. The RCAF required 116 women officers and 4,884 other ranks for trades such as clerks, technicians, and radar or communications operators. Its reserve component needed qualified clerks, switchboard operators, stenographers and other categories traditionally filled by women in civilian society. Air force staff anticipated

that recruiting the required number would take approximately two years.

The army set a much higher goal for its recruitment of women, calling for 236 officers and 8,614 other ranks. Most were to serve in reserve anti-aircraft units — a role found suitable in British wartime experience — while others would replace men in trades such as radar and switchboard operators, clerks, stenographers, dispatch riders and supply personnel.

By comparison, the RCN set rather modest goals. Naval staff estimated that six female officers would be required to act as advisors to the Naval Board on matters relating to the employment of women. A further 50 officers and 450 other ranks were deemed necessary for the technical and non-technical tasks that women would perform during wartime, all as members of naval reserve divisions.

Conditions of service for servicewomen established in the early 1950s removed some of the wartime inequities. Single male and female personnel were to receive the same basic pay but *only single* female personnel were to be accepted: married women could not enlist. The initial engagement for women was limited to three years, in contrast to the five-year term for men.

On 21 March 1951 Cabinet authorized the enlistment of women into the regular RCAF. Former officers and non-commissioned members of the wartime RCAF (WD) or CWAC took on planning and training duties in the re-created organization. The Chief of Air Staff initially allowed the recruitment of women for service in radar units within the Pinetree Line only. This system of radar stations established to detect enemy bombers required a relatively large number of military personnel. Nearly 2,600 women, both officers and airwomen, joined the RCAF (WD) in 1951. Two years later, air force staff decided to recruit more women, for a wider range of occupations. July 1953 marked the high point for the postwar WD, with 3,133 airwomen in service. Thereafter, the establishment was reduced, and by 1954 fewer than a thousand women were wearing air force blue. During this same period the RCAF opened its reserve force to women and recruited a much smaller number than in the regular component. From a high of 1,700 all ranks in 1951–52, the number of reserve airwomen dropped to 511 the following year and then stabilized at about four hundred.

In 1951 approximately a thousand women enlisted in the reserve component of the army. This figure declined over the next two years, to a low of 701, before rising to 1,307 in 1954. In January 1952 the Army Policy Committee weighed the benefits of employing military women versus their civilian counterparts, using the same arguments made during the Second World War.

Servicewomen, the Committee reported, were subject to "greater disciplinary control" than civilians. They could also be posted when and where needed, allowing for the release of men required for field service. According to commonly held expectations, women would serve in the military during any future conflict and thus a peacetime organization would act as the nucleus for expansion. Against these factors were the high cost of servicewomen compared to civilian personnel, the need for additional training facilities and "additional administrative over-head such as housing, clothing and personnel administration." The report's conclusion, that the employment of women "should be basically to release male military personnel where the per capita cost is relatively equal or where civilians are unobtainable," set the course.

In July 1953 a memorandum recommended that women be enrolled in the regular army in order to supply clerical assistance to units in the reserve force. On 1 January 1954 Cabinet gave its authorization and established a limit of 90 female personnel, far fewer than the 215 declared necessary in the July 1953 memorandum. The first women to serve in the regular army were all officers; the other ranks formed a "mobilization reserve" that could be called out on full service if required. With the demands they had to meet in the early stages of the Cold War, army staff needed to have at their disposal all possible "*manpower* as such." Because the number of female soldiers was counted against the overall number of soldiers authorized, the army did not recruit any women into the regular force.

In May 1951 Cabinet authorized the creation of a WRCNS as part of the RCN reserve, but this postwar organization was an integral part of the navy, rather than a separate entity. During its first year 369 officers and female other ranks joined, and in the following year the total climbed to 410. In 1953–54 the strength of the WRCNS declined to 299, but in 1954–55 it rose again, to 349. Many of the women who made up this initial force were employed full-time to meet personnel shortfalls in the Communications Branch, though they remained technically in the reserve. Under this arrangement, however, they could give 30 days' notice and terminate their service. Such relaxed terms of service had the potential to exacerbate any personnel shortages — particularly in times of emergency.

On 26 January 1955 Cabinet authorized the RCN to recruit women directly into its regular component. Naval staff set a ceiling of four hundred female personnel and added two further conditions: women were to be employed only in trades where they would not reduce men's career prospects, and only in trades where they would not adversely affect the ratio of service at sea and on shore. The latter provision referred to the length of time a sailor would spend at sea versus the length of time he would be posted to a land station.

By including women as an integral part of the naval service, this decision set a precedent for all Commonwealth navies. However, integration did not mean equality, and for many naval women going to sea remained only a dream. Petty Officer 2nd Class Eleanor Nichols remarked with regret: "I think I would have liked to have served at sea, but unfortunately there's no positions." It would be many years before that dream became a reality.

The Korean War, 1950–53

It should be remembered that the re-creation of the women's organizations took place against the background of the United Nations Operations in Korea, 1950–53, commonly known as the Korean War. Canadian sailors, airmen and, ultimately, soldiers were sent to the Pacific where they joined the military forces of other nations in what was the first test of the ability of the newly formed United Nations to ensure collective security. This so-called police action provided an opportunity for Canadian women to once again render a valuable service to their nation.

The only Canadian servicewomen to actually serve in the Pacific were the nurses, who as a rule were posted to the theatre for one year, serving six months in Japan and six in Korea. In March 1951 the government committed itself to providing

WRCN Radar Plotters D.L. Morrison, H.R. Ward and P.M. Fotheringham participate in Air Station Familiarization for Maritime Warfare School at HMCS *Shearwater*, 3 November 1955. (NAC, PA 146271)

staff for a four-hundred-bed British Commonwealth hospital. Accordingly, eight nurses were sent as part of the medical group of the Canadian army, which arrived in Kure, Japan, in July 1951. In September 1952 the first Commonwealth nursing sisters arrived in Seoul. The task of the six nurses — two each from Canada, Australia and Britain — was to set up a one-hundred-bed hospital in an old school. The British Commonwealth Communications Zone Medical Unit, as it was called, certainly had humble beginnings. Supplies were alternately very scarce and over-abundant. Necessary repairs had to be carried out with patients in-situ, and the canvas cots were so low that treating a patient often required the nurses to kneel on the earthen floor. Conditions were in sharp contrast to those in Canadian hospitals, but through the hard work of the nurses and other personnel the patients received proper care and much was made of the way all concerned worked together to meet the challenges.

In a letter reprinted in *The Military Nurses of Canada,* Major Elizabeth B. Neil described conditions in Seoul:

> *The outside of the buildings looks quite respectable, but inside is not too good. Plaster falls from the ceilings, and they tell me that when it rains I will need an umbrella in my office. Our quarters have possibilities, but at present are very bare. We have a bed each, some nails on which to hang our clothes, a bucket latrine.*

In the same book, Captain Dorothy Doyle recalls the innovative and cooperative spirit not just of the medical officers but of all staff. For example, steam tables were created from oil drums and M-37 burners, and the supply

people never turned up at the hospital without bringing something of use.

The all-male No. 25 Canadian Field Dressing Station was the next unit to be opened to nursing officers. This 112-bed station, located some 30 kilometres north of Seoul, consisted of prefabricated huts and handled all but the

RCAF policewoman checks identification at the gate, circa 1950. (RCN 54 (29))

most serious cases. In the two weeks following the armistice, more than a thousand Commonwealth soldiers who had been prisoners of war passed through No. 25. After a shower and the issue of a new uniform, they were given a medical examination, inoculations and a hearty meal. The dressing station remained in Korea until late 1954, treating patients for sickness and accidental injury.

The aeromedical training received by some RCAF nurses proved invaluable during the Korean War. A number of nurses were also attached to the United States Air Force and cared for casualties on flights from Japan to San Francisco, while others participated in Canada's first large-scale hospital airlift in the summer of 1951. On this occasion, Canadian casualties who had been transported to Tacoma, Washington, by the USAF were taken in a converted Dakota air ambulance to DVA hospitals in Canada. After the signing of the armistice, some of the nurses attended to released prisoners of war as they were being flown back to Canada.

As always, serving as part of an allied effort provided opportunities for sharing the peculiarities of one's national military service. In *The Military Nurses of Canada*, Flight Lieutenant Isabel Ziegler describes an incident that occurred while she was serving as an air-evacuation nurse on board an American aircraft:

> *...as I was going down the aisle with special diets, a Canadian patient called to me. He got as far as "Oh Sister" when my [American] medical assistant told him in no uncertain terms that he was speaking to an officer. He was to call her by her rank or say ma'am, definitely not sister. I just caught him by the arm and quietly explained our tradition in the Commonwealth countries of referring to us as nursing sisters. Far from it being a derogatory term, we much preferred it to being addressed by our rank. He was very embarrassed, but it did point out one of our differences.*

Military Nursing, 1948–59

It was throughout the immediate postwar period that nurses saw the most widespread service. While military operations in Korea were still in progress, nurses with the RCAMC and the RCAF were serving as part of Canada's contribution to North Atlantic Treaty Organization (NATO) forces in Europe.

Between 1951 and 1953 the RCAF deployed four fighter wings to Europe to make up 1st Canadian Air Division. Eventually two were located in France at Grostenquin and Marville, and two in West Germany at Zweibrucken and Baden-Soellingen. Nursing sisters served at all of these, the main hospital being at Zweibrucken, where 20 were posted. The other three wings had infirmaries employing between six and eight nurses each. The occasional crash during flying training added to the number of patients requiring more than routine care. As with army nurses, these women, who served for two years under a rotation policy, were also responsible for the care of service families.

In November 1953, 27 Canadian Infantry Brigade Group took over four newly constructed camps near the city of Soest, Germany, marking the first permanent Canadian Army presence in Europe. The main hospital at Iserlohn, a very short distance away, was run by the British Royal Army Medical Corps but staffed jointly by Canadian and British personnel. Clinics were also eventually established at each of the camps, staffed by up to three nursing sisters. Public health nursing for the soldiers' families was included among their duties, although the maternity ward at Iserlohn was staffed solely by the British.

Nurses who served in Korea could, after a posting at one of the military hospitals in Canada, find themselves sent overseas again, to care for members of the brigade group in West Germany, while air force nurses might also be posted to any of the various stations that housed the squadrons of 1st Canadian Air Division in France and West Germany.

Back in Canada, once air evacuation training resumed, more women each year took the required course. Subjects included meteorology, communications, ditching and survival, as well as all aspects of aeromedical work with an emphasis on the ability to swim and survive a crash at sea. Not surprisingly, immunity to air sickness was tested during periods of stunt flying with the candidates continuing to attend to their "patients" — in this instance, other nurses. Isabel Ziegler confesses in *The Military Nurses of Canada* that she wanted to be a pilot when she joined the RCAF but had to content herself with being a nurse, although she was lucky enough to be chosen for aeromedical evacuation training. "Each nurse had certain preferences," Ziegler says, "most were hoping to do something where they would move by air."

In 1951 RCAF nurses entered the exciting and dangerous field of para-rescue, which until then had been restricted to airmen and doctors. At the Para-Rescue School in Edmonton, candidates had to face six weeks of rigorous physical training and classroom instruction before attempting their first parachute jump. After mastering the basics of jumping, they moved on to Henry House

Para-rescue nurses, 6 April 1955. (CFPU, PC 676)

Field at Jasper to gain practical experience in "parachute jumps to open and timbered country, mountain and glacier climbing, survival techniques and shelter building, and first aid and evacuation of injured." As one of the original group broke her leg during a jump, only four nurses qualified for the para-rescue badge. The nurses then returned to their duties in the station hospital, to be called from their day-to-day work when circumstances required their special skills.

In a related field, the postwar period saw a significant decline in the number of dietitians serving with the RCAMC. By 1959 the shortage was so acute that the army obtained permission to sponsor graduates with degrees in home economics and household science for further training and internships. Once they had finished their training and internship, they were required to serve for a minimum period in the regular force.

On 1 January 1959, in a foreshadowing of the eventual total force unification, the medical services of the three armed forces were integrated into the Canadian Forces Medical Service, headed by the Surgeon-General.

The nursing service was one of the components of the new organization, although candidates still joined the service of their choice and wore the appropriate uniform. They enlisted for a "short service commission" of between two and five years, after which they could apply for an extension or a permanent commission.

Commander Glynis Elliott, who had been a member of the WRCNS but had served primarily with the army, found that little transition was required, because nurses from the three services had already served together on various postings in Canada and Europe as a matter of course.

For her, the only change worth noting was the eventual adoption of a single uniform. Integration increased the number of places to which women could be posted, including the National Defence Medical Centre in Ottawa, which opened in October 1961, and the types of nursing they might be required to perform.

The Decline of Women's Participation in the Services, 1955–65

In the late 1950s a number of factors combined to reduce the number of women in military service and cloud their future. In 1955 the Air Council lowered the maximum number of airwomen to 2,500 from the 1953–54 ceiling of four thousand. The air force staff stated that the smaller number was in line with recruiting capabilities, although as late as July 1953 there were 3,133 women in the RCAF. As experience with women in uniform increased, the RCAF also identified a number of problems related to female personnel. Chief among these was the relatively short average length of service by airwomen. This had a particularly great impact given that competency levels in the increasingly sophisticated technical trades required longer training periods and more time. Ultimately, airwomen were prevented from entering trades that required more than 16 weeks of training. The perceived physical limitations of women also garnered criticism, but there were other, not openly reported, factors that might have led to a high attrition rate — little mention was made of the fact that the early WDs were sometimes posted to stations that "were neither prepared to accommodate them nor to gainfully employ them in their trades." The morale of airwomen also suffered because of the quality and limited availability of various items of uniform.

In 1962, when the Pinetree Line was replaced by SAGE (semi-automated ground environment), a system that relied more heavily on computers and consequently required fewer personnel, the WD component was reduced in size. Given that the functioning of the earlier system had played a large part in the decision to recreate the Division, the decision to forego recruiting women for two years came as no surprise. A 1963 study to determine the future need for women in the RCAF foresaw the requirement for an establishment of only 1,100 personnel, and in June 1964 the Chief of Air Staff concluded that even this number was too high and decided to "phase out" female personnel. The Minister of National Defence asked that this action be delayed and requested a briefing on the current and proposed policy regarding the employment of women in all three services.

In 1955 the army, for its part, began recruiting personnel for the CWAC to serve as nursing assistants, a non-medical corps trade. These women had been providing care for the families of soldiers, particularly on isolated stations, but by 1963 this need had greatly diminished and recruiting ceased. Those already in uniform fulfilled all predictable requirements, and by the end of 1965 there were only 29 nursing assistants and nine CWAC officers serving in the regular army.

The RCN had only 55 women serving in 1955, but the number had risen to 140 by 1961 when "the position of WRCNS in the personnel structure of the RCN" came under review. In the course of the study, one of the options considered was the dissolution of the organization. A committee formed to look into this matter recommended that female officers be recruited and employed in specialized capacities; that Wrens continue to be employed in the communications, supply, medical and operational fields; that women

cease to serve in Pacific Command; and that the conditions of service for the women of the RCN mirror as closely as possible those of the men.

The Naval Board accepted this advice. In 1962 a shortage in the Communications Branch was so severe that additional women had to be recruited. While initially there were concerns about the effect on the male members of the radioman trade, the shorter terms of women's service meant that their numbers could be reduced quickly if the shortage proved temporary. The WRCNS underwent yet another review in 1964, under the guise of the Personnel Structure Review Team (Landymore Report). While the general conclusions indicated that women in the navy were rendering good service, new conditions were set for their future deployment. Naval women, the report recommended, should be used only for positions in which "men cannot be suitably or effectively employed and where civilians possessed of the required skills were not obtainable" and in trades where personnel shortages existed, but only "for temporary employment until the trade resumes its normal strength." These conditions appeared to reduce RCN servicewomen to near auxiliary status, making them secondary to the men rather than equal members of their service.

By 1965 the future of women in the armed forces had become uncertain. From its distinction of being the first service to recruit women in the Second World War and the last to release them, the RCAF had again claimed pride of place by being the first to re-create its women's organization. Yet by 1964 it wished to eliminate the WD in its entirety and had only 566 officers and airwomen serving, a significant drop from a high of more than three thousand. The RCN headcount consisted of only 288 female officers and other ranks, who, after the Landymore Report, seemed at risk of being reduced to a mere appendage of their service, while the CWAC, always smaller, had just 38 regular force members.

Ironing room in Conestoga Building where WRCNS members prepare uniforms for inspection, HMCS *Cornwallis*, 13 November 1963. (EKS 1430)

Captain Jane Foster, one of the first women to train as a fighter
pilot, in the cockpit of a CF-5, 2 November 1988.
(CFPU, CKC 88-6230)

Chapter IV

AN EVER WIDENING ROLE: 1965–88

Even though they had accomplished much, women's service in the military was again called into question two decades after the end of the Second World War. Their continuing presence in the military and the expansion of their role was precipitated by external forces, including the political influence exerted by the Minister of National Defence, the Royal Commission of 1971, the *Canadian Human Rights Act* of 1978 and, ultimately, the 1982 *Charter of Rights and Freedoms*.

The Minister's Manpower Study, 1965

Following the decision to exclude women from the air force, the Defence Minister's Manpower Study, which was commissioned in 1964, made a comprehensive examination of the role of women in the armed forces. The three services were canvassed concerning potential roles for female officers and enlisted personnel, and Department of Labour studies were also reviewed. The results showed that women were more and more likely to be part of the civilian work force, in which their participation was increasing at a rate faster than that of their male counterparts. Banning them from service in the armed forces would clearly, therefore, be out of step with the broader economic and social trends in Canada, and indeed the study stressed that "the privilege of serving their country in the armed forces should not be denied on the grounds of sex alone."

Jobs commonly held by women in the civilian world dovetailed with their proposed employment in the services, with clerical tasks predominating. A list of trades to be opened to women was compiled and categorized according to whether women were "essential," "preferable" or "equally suitable" to men. As nursing assistants and flight attendants, women were judged to be uniquely suited; as clerks they were expected to outperform men; and as medical or dental assistants and supply technicians they were seen to be equal to men. The principles espoused in 1951, when the women's services were re-established, would remain in place: servicewomen were not to replace civilians unless the employment of civilians was impractical or uneconomical, and the employment of women was not to significantly affect the rotation ratio of men serving on isolated or sea duty.

The Minister's Manpower Study debunked some of the long-held objections to servicewomen. While it was argued by many that the employment of women was expensive and brought with it a particular administrative burden, the study countered that few of these challenges were neither insurmountable nor based on solid facts. For example, a shortage of uniforms was easily resolved and the cost of adapting accommodation could be reduced by employing a minimum number of women at a particular location. The cost of housing servicewomen was actually found to be lower, because a large percentage of men were married with children and in need of a subsistence allowance or married quarters, schools and other dependents' facilities. The only criticism considered valid was the cost of illegitimate pregnancies, as the armed forces had to provide additional medical care and a cash allowance when pregnant women left the service, but the incidence of pregnancy was low enough to be regarded as a minor concern.

The most well-founded objection to the employment of servicewomen was their high rate of attrition compared to men, so that, if recruiting and training costs for the two sexes were the same, the "cost" of employing a woman would still be higher. A number of variables served to lessen this cost differential, not the least of which was the fact that women were essential in certain occupations, making a cost comparison irrelevant. Nevertheless, the attrition rate of servicewomen was felt to be high enough to warrant their restriction to trades that required limited training.

As for the advantages, servicewomen were seen as representing "force flexibility." When the armed forces were unable to draw sufficient personnel from their traditional male sources, women could quickly be recruited for trades requiring less training and men could be released for more complex tasks. Both the navy and the air force had already drawn from the female "manpower pool" for communications personnel and air defence system personnel, respectively. Another positive factor in the employment of women was their ability to respond quickly to new postings. Apart from emergencies or certain trades in which quick transfers could be expected, servicemen, many of whom were married with families, had to be given adequate notice of posting. Servicewomen, on the other hand, were almost always single and could be "moved with less notice, expense and personal difficulty." This benefit, however, could be exploited only by those trades

Navigator with
437 Squadron
aboard a 707, 1987.
(CFPU, ISC 87-319)

Master Seaman Pierre Gendron
and Corporal S. Thompson hauling
in rope as HMCS *Cormorant* comes
alongside the Dartmouth Slips
during the SWINTER trials, 1980.
(CFPU, IHC 80-493)

Corporal Sue Kinney
of 409 Squadron removes
chock from around CF-18
wheel during a Tactical Air
Meet in Kleine Brogel,
Belgium, 23 June–3 July
1986. (CFPU, ILC 86-83)

Female officer cadet in Parade Square, Royal Military College, Kingston, Ontario, 22 September 1980. (CFPU, IOC 80-133)

Officer cadet inspection by Drill Instructor Master Warrant Officer Tripp, Royal Military College, Kingston, 22 September 1980. (CFPU, IOC 80-136)

and units in which women were present in numbers.

Since women would not be permitted to serve at isolated stations or in operational units that could be sent to the world's trouble spots, the study concluded that men might have to serve somewhat longer periods in these locations. When the forces needed to be reduced, however, servicewomen would provide a degree of adaptability; because they traditionally served for shorter periods, an overall force reduction would not necessitate the release of men who wished to remain in service. This was not to suggest, the report stressed, that women who also wished to continue in service should be forced out. In the final analysis, a cadre of service-women would lay the foundation for flexibility simply by providing the basis for expansion whenever this outcome was desired.

Serving women were certainly aware that they were seen as more flexible and mobile than servicemen — in fact, some thought they were perceived almost as "spare parts." Commander Glynis Elliott, a nurse who served from the mid-1960s to 1990, recalls that single women living in quarters could be posted at a week's notice, and often were. "You were posted any time of the year at very short notice to wherever they had a need because you had no great furniture. That's why I got posted from Victoria to Borden between Christmas and New Year." The treatment would not have differed greatly for single men, but the nature of women's service was that they remained single for most or all of their careers.

The overall conclusion of the Minister's Manpower Study in 1965 was that the decision of the Royal Canadian Air Force to

Nurses on leave in Paris, 1968. (CFPU, RE 68-6146)

dissolve its Women's Division was unsound. Among other things, the study recommended that the "requirement for women in uniform be recognized as permanent, and not subject to further review in principle." The navy, army and air force were directed to recruit women according to the list of trades for which they were deemed essential, preferred or equally suitable. New occupational categories were not to be opened to women, however, without a review to ensure that men would not be subject to unacceptable rotation ratios. The design and supply of women's uniforms were identified as needing atten-tion, but the terms of engagement, career policy and other administrative questions relating to servicewomen were to be settled after completion of a larger manpower report on the armed forces as a whole.

Unification, 1968, and the Royal Commission on the Status of Women, 1971

On 1 February 1968 the Royal Canadian Navy, Canadian Army and Royal Canadian Air Force were unified to form the Canadian Forces (CF). With unification, the Canadian Women's Air Corps, Women's Royal Canadian Naval Service and RCAF (WD) were eliminated, but the status of their members was essentially unchanged; they simply became part of the unified CF.

Much debate and interest were generated by the creation of the new single-service uniform. In May 1968 *Sentinel* magazine reported that the women's dress uniforms would be "chic, military and happily feminine." Before being issued widely, however, the proposed uniforms were tested by personnel in a variety of environments. On the whole, the prototypes shown in *Sentinel* and other publications were not the exact uniforms eventually issued. The exception was the uniform of nursing officers, which remained unchanged, "with the addition of the traditional veil, their white stockings and shoes."

Three years after unification, the Royal Commission on the Status of Women concluded its study on the place of women in Canadian society. Of its 167 recommendations, six had direct implications for the CF. The report recommended the following changes: that enlistment criteria and pension benefits be standardized; that married women

be allowed to enlist; that pregnancy not necessitate termination of service; that women be given the opportunity to attend military colleges; and that all trades and classifications be open to women.

The armed forces adopted all but the last recommendation. The Defence Council nevertheless established a new employment policy on 5 July 1971 stating that there were to be no limitations on the employment of women in the CF other than those imposed by the following factors:

- *Maintenance of the capacity to perform the military role defined in Canadian defence policy within the concept of "forces in being";*

- *The acceptance of Canadian and western society of the employment of women in direct support of military operations in support of this policy; and*

- *The necessity of providing job rotation and career development for male members for whom a significant proportion of their postings are in combat support, remote units or at sea.*

As the years passed, the number of trades closed to servicewomen was gradually reduced and the enlistment of women increased. In 1971 there was a personnel ceiling of 1,500; 15 years later the actual number of women serving was more than five times that figure.

The 1971 annual report of the Department of National Defence (DND) concluded that the effects of the Royal Commission would be to make a wider range of career opportunities open to women and raise their number as recruitment increased and specialist and trades courses became available. Women were now eligible for the Reserve

Private Heather J. MacDonald replaces rivets at CFB Baden, West Germany, during the SWINTER trials, 1980. (BSC 80-1093)

Corporal Nicole Maksemiuk repairs the motor on a projector at CFB Lahr, West Germany. (CFPU, PCN 80-203)

Leading Wren Henia Malinowski, a diesel technician, tends to a diesel engine of HMCS Carleton's YFL 104 "Pogo," Ottawa, 15 May 1986. (CFPU, ISC 86-311)

Officer Training Plan, the Medical Officers' Training Plan, the Dental Officers' Program, the University Training Plan for Men and the University Training Plan for Officers. They were, however, still not permitted to enter the military colleges because of "the lack of facilities and unsuitability of the type of training available." One example of the "unsuitability" of training for female officer cadets was ceremonial parades, as it was "assumed that rifle drill is unbecoming to females and, moreover, difficult in a physical sense for them to master effectively." In December 1972, DND announced that women would be given the opportunity to compete for positions in 13 officer classifications and 30 trades, although they were still to be excluded from primary combat roles, seagoing duty and service in isolated areas.

From 1971 to 1978 the number of women serving in the armed forces markedly increased. In the reserves, the increase was 18 to 19 per cent, considerably higher than that of the regular force, at between 2 and 7 per cent. An article in the November–December 1971 issue of *Sentinel* heralded a lowering of the ceiling for the employment of women and featured an interview with the outgoing "Queen Bee" — the advisor on women in the forces — Lieutenant-Colonel Lois Davis, and her replacement, Lieutenant-Colonel Mary Vallance. The author reported that while there was much talk about the Royal Commission there was little mention of "Women's Liberation." After summarizing the ways in which the Royal Commission would change the CF, the article emphasized that there were "some trades women will not enter. The combat role is out in our civilization." However, a briefing

note prepared by the Director of the Women's Personnel Service after 1971 spelled out a change in opinion:

We believe the concept of women freeing men for combat duty is outdated. A service-woman's mission is to make available to the Canadian Forces the special skills and abilities she possesses. The CF is a team of professionally dedicated men and women, all of whom perform a necessary function. For the women in the Canadian Forces equal opportunity means equal commitment.

By the mid-1970s women were serving at all major locations in Canada, with North Atlantic Treaty Organization (NATO) forces in Europe and with the United Nations Emergency Force in the Middle East. There were early concerns that the Canadian military would lose credibility in the eyes of its allies and potential enemies and would encounter problems when serving with allies who did not support the concept of women in the armed forces. However, these concerns were assuaged — or at least set aside. The number of officer classifications open to women had now increased to 18 and there were more than twice as many trades in which women could serve. Employment qualifications were the same for all members of the service and the practice of limiting training opportunities for women had been discontinued.

In September 1974 a study was undertaken to determine which positions had to be filled by men because of restrictions on women's service. The Vice-Chief of the Defence Staff identified those positions that were limited to men for operational reasons, while the Assistant Deputy Minister (Personnel) enumerated those that were reserved for men out of personnel considerations — for example, to balance a sea:shore ratio or to allow for career progression. Of all service positions, 39,521 were limited to males and the remaining 29,847 were to be filled by the most qualified candidate regardless of sex. Two thirds of all trades and classifications were now open to both sexes.

Perhaps more important than the rising number of trades and classifications open to women was the increasing representa-

Major (later Major-General) Wendy Clay, a doctor, qualifies for her pilot's wings on 19 August 1974, six years before the pilot trade was opened to all women. (CFPU, MJ 74-1222)

tion of women in non-traditional roles. By 1976 they were represented in 16 of the 18 officer classifications open to them, while enlisted women were serving in 52 of the 64 trades for which they were eligible.

Even though there was no restriction on service, the recruitment of women into

highly technical or journeyman trades was still slow, and servicewomen continued to be concentrated in administration, finance, logistics, medicine and other traditional women's pursuits. Those who did enter other areas "prove to be competent, and their integration and acceptance into former all-male sections is proceeding satisfactorily," according to a report presented at a meeting of the Committee on Women in the NATO Forces in September 1976. Even so, some servicewoman admitted that, while they welcomed the widening range of occupations, they wanted more opportunities still. In a 1980 *Ottawa Citizen* article, Master Corporal Camille Tkacz said she wished to be posted to Germany but was barred from the positions available because they were combat jobs and she was a woman. "But I'm more than willing," she declared. "Take me to a regiment! I want to try it."

The SWINTER Trials, 1979–84

On 1 March 1978 the *Canadian Human Rights Act*, which forbade discrimination on a number of grounds, including gender, became law. There was, however, a provision that allowed employers to exclude certain jobs from the requirements of the Act if they could demonstrate that there was a "bona fide

Private S.A. Clairmont, a vehicle technician, maintains a truck engine, 10 January 1987. (CFPU, ISC 87-13)

Corporal Gaye Toupin, the first woman to join the Skyhawks, the Canadian Forces Parachute team, 1978. (CFPU, IEC 78-481)

occupational requirement" to do so. This legislation caused the CF to examine its personnel policies to determine what changes were required, if any. A study team was created to explore the following factors:

- *Effects of the employment of women on operational effectiveness and efficiency;*

- *Conflicts between individual rights and national security;*

- *Medical aspects, including physical strength;*

- *Differential costs: uniform designs, modifications to accommodations, etc;*

- *Anticipated recruiting difficulties after 1982;*

- *Impact of the present CF employment restrictions;*

- *Perceptions of servicemen, servicewomen, their spouses and the Canadian public;*

- *Employment at isolated posts; and*

- *Eligibility for military colleges.*

Since the Forces could not readily find answers to all these questions, a five-year evaluation program, known as Service Women in Non-Traditional Environments and Roles (SWINTER), was initiated. Its objective was to determine the viability of employing women in near-combat units of all three services, specifically as pilots, at sea, with land force field units and on isolated postings. A "near-combat unit" was defined as one that "may become directly involved in combat but whose primary role is other than combat."

Captains Deanna Brasseur, Leah Mosher and Nora Bottomley — Canada's first women pilot trainees — during the high-attitude indoctrination course at the Canadian Forces School of Aeromedical Training, Winnipeg, February 1980. (IW 80-004)

In November 1979, as part of the SWINTER trials, the first women to serve as pilots began their training at Portage la Prairie, Manitoba. Because of the time required to produce a squadron-ready pilot, this trial lasted until October 1985. The first woman pilot in the CF was actually Major Wendy Clay, a medical officer, who had received her wings six years earlier in order to better understand her patients, but the 1979 trainees were the first to prepare for service in transport, search and rescue, and training roles.

In 1981 *Sentinel* ran an article on the first three servicewomen to receive their pilot's wings. The news media and the general public saw these trailblazers as somewhat exotic. They were subjected to repeated questions and to attention that could be trying at times. There were other tensions as well. Captain Deanna Brasseur explained that the three felt isolated from their male counterparts; interestingly, she attributed this to age difference — as most of the men were younger officer cadets and second-lieutenants — and to the attention the women received. Captain Leah Mosher described the pressure they were under as "the first" and the challenge of focusing on the job at hand. For Captain Nora Bottomley the greatest pressure was internal: her desire to succeed and the effort she expended to do so.

In all, 40 women pilots were trained and posted to operational flying units where they proved themselves capable and were integrated into near-combat aviation roles. Women were also being employed as

Master Corporal Wilma Carroll stands watch aboard HMCS *Cormorant* while Leading Seaman Al Boudreau flashes the "9" signal light, during the SWINTER trials, 25 September 1980. (CFPU, IHC 80-492)

operational aircrew on a trial basis. At the end of the aircrew trial, general acceptance and support for the continued and expanded employment of women was evident, but despite this, and despite a clear demonstration of ability, Air Command decided against the continued use of women because of the restrictions on their ability to fly. In the Command's opinion, a pilot who could not be called upon to fly combat or near-combat missions was not a full participant in Canada's air force. If the decision was taken to employ female pilots, however, the Commander of Air Command recommended that "no restriction be placed on their employment."

Land force SWINTER trials, involving service in Germany with 4 Service Battalion and 4 Field Ambulance of 4 Canadian Mechanized Brigade Group, were also begun. The former unit provided supply, transport and maintenance support; the latter provided frontline treatment and evacuation of casualties for the brigade. Approximately 60 positions in the service battalion and approximately 15 in the field ambulance were filled by women, and the trial, which ended in September 1984, concluded that properly selected and trained women could do the required work but that their employment impaired operational effectiveness.

From 1980 to 1984 the navy carried out a SWINTER sea trial aboard the fleet-diving tender HMCS *Cormorant,* a non-combatant ship. Between eight and 13 women were part of the ship's company during this four-year period, and, to simplify staffing, those selected served in the support occupations for which they were already qualified. This particular test demonstrated that non-combatant vessels could easily hold mixed-gender crews and that female crew members could effectively carry out their duties, although complete integration of the ship's company did not occur. The navy concluded that servicewomen were regarded as suitable for posting to "minor war vessels such as patrol boats, gate vessels and small training vessels."

Women were also sent to Canadian Forces Station Alert, an isolated posting previously closed to them. Duty in the high Arctic required adaptation to harsh weather conditions "with little relief from alternating spells of high activity on the job and restricted opportunity for normal travel off duty." In the Alert trial, servicewomen filled about 20 positions for six months at a time, over a period of three years. Those employed were drawn from support trades such as clerks, supply technicians and cooks. This part of the study, concluded in 1983, resulted in the employment of servicewomen at isolated locations on the same basis as their male counterparts.

Not surprisingly, there was disagreement on the wisdom of placing women in near-combat roles. In a 1981 *Sentinel* article, Lieutenant-Colonel Carl Fitzpatrick offered a tongue-in-cheek description of the reaction to the first female pilot trainees. "For a while in late 1979, NORAD [North American Aerospace Defence Command] spotters could have been forgiven had they reported small, fuzzy UFOs high over the western Canadian landscape. That's about how high some eyebrows were raised when the first batch of tradition-breaking women arrived on the doorstep of No. 3 Canadian Forces Flying Training School, CFB Portage la Prairie,

Man., to begin — gulp — pilot training." On the other hand, Lieutenant-Commander Gil Morrison, captain of HMCS *Cormorant,* had little time for those (especially retired naval members) who opposed the presence of women on ships. As he explained in an interview with Southam News: "You don't drive down the highway looking through the rear-view mirror. You consult it, but you look ahead." Morrison acknowledged that the men currently serving under him aboard *Cormorant* were likely to have difficulty accepting women doing jobs that had been theirs. They might, he suggested "feel their toes are being stepped on, and that's understandable," but "after the initial shock period is over, they'll get on with the job."

Not all concerns were so lighthearted or personal. A report prepared by the Canadian Forces Personnel Applied Research Unit, which examined the scientific methodology behind the SWINTER trials, identified three factors that had the potential to affect many of the variables associated with unit operational effectiveness. These were: "the placement of women into unfamiliar environmental and operational conditions; their performance of new employments; and their introduction into previously all-male settings." The Unit's scientists were not advising against the employment of women in near-combat units, but merely identifying the need to account for these factors when planning the next stage of integration.

A 1978 survey of the attitudes of military members of both sexes, their spouses and the general public also addressed possible drawbacks to increasing female participation. To varying degrees, survey participants

Female officer with Colours of Collège Militaire Royal at the graduation of the first class to include women cadets, Saint-Jean, Quebec, May 1985. (CFPU, IMC 85-340)

military colleges, in practice women had been given access only to education support programs in civilian universities. It was not until 1980 that the Collège Militaire Royale in Saint-Jean, Quebec, and the Royal Military College in Kingston, Ontario, welcomed their first "lady officer cadets," and it was 1984 before the first such "lady cadets" entered Royal Roads Military College in Esquimalt, British Columbia. At first there were misgivings on the part of some college alumni, military personnel and even the general public, but these diminished over time.

The Hundredth Anniversary of Canadian Women in Service: A Snapshot of 1985

The 1985 annual report for DND summarized the progress made since women had first entered military service as nurses during the North-West Rebellion. Within NATO, only the United States had a higher percentage of females in its armed forces, and proud reference was made to the range of classifications and trades open to women, the equality of terms and conditions of service, and the promotion opportunities. The author of the report acknowledged that the number of women in senior positions was limited but noted that their presence was increasing with the passage of time.

The personnel services organizations were much more cautious in their approach to the centenary. A memo dated 14 May 1984 warned that "before we joyously plunge into this 100th year anniversary we should pause to assess how far we have come in our treatment of women in the Canadian Forces." There was thought to be "a certain irony" in

identified "physical capabilities, marital conflict, the emotional suitability of women and the impact of women on operational capabilities." Of these drawbacks, women in the CF believed that marital conflict was the only difficult or possibly insoluble one. One interesting result of the survey was that while a clear majority of spouses believed that women had the "capabilities to perform in combat roles, they generally [did] not think that women should have the opportunity to do so nor did they wish to see their spouse with the opposite sex in combat roles except as aircrew."

Although the 1971 Royal Commission had called for the admission of women to the

**UNIFORMS
1941 – 90**

A member of the RCAF (WD).
which was formed in 1941.
(Re-creation by Ronald B. Vo   Global)

VOLSTAD85

A member of the CWAC,
Italy, 1943–44. (Re-creation
by Ronald B. Volstad, Art Global)

VOLSTAD95

A member of the WRCNS in 1942.
(Re-creation by Ronald B. Volstad, Art Global)

VOLSTAD 94

Servicewomen from each of the three
services shortly before unification of
the CF and adoption of the single-
service uniform, Halifax, 1968.
(CFPU, REC 68-881)

Servicewomen from each of the three services wearing Distinct
Environmental Uniforms after abandonment of the single-service
uniform, Halifax, 4 May 1990. (CFPU, HSC 90-439-1)

the fact that the SWINTER trials — to see if women were fit for near-combat roles — were concluding a century after 12 nurses had served in a theatre of operations that was primitive and, "relative to the state of the warfare of the day, posed some danger to the nurses." A temperate approach to the celebration was counselled in order to avoid embarrassment at the lack of progress in certain areas. Given the media attention that the milestone would bring, Major-General Borden R. Campbell warned that DND "should be prepared to deal with all aspects of women in the CF both the bright spots as well as the contentious issues." He suggested that the "corps of nurses" would be a good focal point.

The CREW Trials, 1987–89

In April 1985 the "Equality Rights" section of the *Canadian Charter of Rights and Freedoms* came into effect. This document asserted the "right to the equal protection and equal benefit of the law without discrimination and, in particular, without discrimination" based on gender. In October 1985 the Parliamentary Sub-Committee on Equality Rights recommended that "all trades and occupations in the Canadian Armed Forces be open to women." In March 1986 the government tabled a response, promising to pursue an expansion of roles for women provided operational effectiveness would not be adversely affected. A Charter Task Force was appointed, and its recommendations resulted in more military occupations being opened to women and a call for further study to examine the

possibility of dropping even more gender barriers.

In order to test how increased equality would affect the armed forces, the Combat-Related Employment of Women (CREW) trials were announced on 5 February 1987. Their purpose was to "evaluate the impact of mixed-gender units on operational effectiveness." Thus far, women had been prevented from serving with air force tactical helicopter and fighter squadrons; with army infantry, artillery, armour, field engineer, field signals and field intelligence units; and, within the navy, service in the destroyer fleet, which

Lieutenant-General J.J. Paradis, commander of Mobile Command, enrolling France Archambault, one of the first female cadets at Collège Militaire Royal in Saint-Jean, Quebec, 27 June 1980. (CFPU, IM 80-128)

represented some 80 per cent of the seagoing positions. Now, the last bastions of male service were evaluated and women were recruited for the first time into the "hard sea" trades and combat arms. Even service in submarines with their limited accommodation and hygiene facilities was to be considered.

In June 1987 the air force announced that it did not need to participate in the trial and immediately removed all restrictions on the

Air Defence technician operating a radar scope in the Regional Operations Control Centre in the underground complex of the NORAD installation at CFB North Bay, 13 March 1987. (CFPU, ISC 87-224)

employment of servicewomen. Women were to be admitted to all trades and classifications, including fighter pilots, navigators and flight engineers, and the first two female pilots began fighter aircraft training in the spring of 1988.

The army and navy began posting servicewomen into combat units in 1987 and proceeded on a phased-in basis. Sufficient numbers of men and women were to be employed in these trial units so as to provide both mutual support for either gender and at the same time "to have the potential to put stress on the cohesiveness of the unit as a whole." There was an expectation that "unit cohesion would suffer if, over time, the women are found to be significantly weaker or to have less stamina and endurance than their male peers, or if social pairing off of men and women within the group occurs and interferes with the ability of the group to work together in stressful situations on a professional basis."

As servicewomen entered nontraditional areas, they faced challenges in gaining the acceptance of their male peers and in proving equal to the rigours of their assigned tasks. In a 1988 article in *Sentinel,* Private Kris Berg gave a personal account of a parachute course she had taken. As the only woman among 57 men, she had "wondered how the men would react to my presence, but it wasn't [my] main concern." Private Berg had been far more concerned with her ability to pass the physical and mental tests that faced her.

Another concern raised at this time was the spectre of atrocities committed against women taken as prisoners of war. In an eloquent letter published in the Spring 1988 issue of *Canadian Defence Quarterly,* a serving officer reminded readers that "the conventions, treaties and human rights declarations

Artillery Spotter taking notes during a field exercise,
1975. (CFPU, REC 75-694)

Corporal Joanna Gilkinson soldering capacitors on an emergency VHF unit at
CFB Baden, West Germany, during the SWINTER trials, 22 June 1980.
(CFPU, BSC 80-1091)

which are supposed to apply" in wartime often did not, and he asked whether society would "permit a government to allow large numbers of Canadian women to be subjected to such treatment."

The trial service of women in the land and sea forces was set to continue through 1989, with an analysis to follow, but before it was concluded the CF were once again forced to adapt to a major external influence.

Lieutenant Svendson of 709 Communications Regiment speaks on a radio during a field exercise, 9 June 1990. (CFPU, IOC, 90-9-38/40)

Chapter V

TOWARDS A NEW CENTURY: 1988–99

...we must now accept that there no longer exists a *bona fide* occupational requirement for discrimination against women through employment limitations.

— General Paul D. Manson, Chief of the Defence Staff, 1989

As Canadian society changes so too must the Army. It must reflect the values of society or risk losing its support. That's why obstacles to the integration of women in the combat arms is a deep concern of mine...
Also, I am making it clear, he who does not understand or fully support the right of women to serve equally with men in today's Army has no place in the Army's chain of command.

— Lieutenant-General J. Maurice Baril, Chief of the Land Staff, 1997

A Decade of Change and Growth

As the 1980s drew to a close, the Canadian Human Rights Commission (CHRC) lowered the last barriers for women in the Canadian Forces (CF). The decade that followed may be divided into three phases: the initial opening of all trades and occupations; the shift in focus caused by fiscal restraint; and a renewed interest in gender integration. In the Gulf War and in a growing number of peace-keeping missions abroad, Canadian service-women proved themselves capable of meeting challenges as equals.

The Ruling of the Canadian Human Rights Commission Tribunal, 1989

In response to complaints from four servicewomen and one serviceman, the CHRC convened a tribunal to carry out an investigation. The women alleged that they had been denied employment based on gender, while the man claimed reverse discrimination because he was required to fly in combat while women were not. To illustrate the rapid pace of change in these matters, the occupational category that one of the women was trying to enter was opened to both sexes before the tribunal made its ruling. For the others, the tribunal undertook to determine whether bona fide occupational requirements existed to prevent women from serving in all aspects of the military.

The tribunal held hearings, visited units, consulted military and civilian experts, and gathered information from other nations. On 20 February 1989 it ruled that any obstacles to the entry of servicewomen into all occupations had to be lifted, with two exceptions: service on submarines and service in the Roman Catholic chaplaincy. In particular, the tribunal ordered:

- *The CAF CREW [Canadian Armed Forces Combat Related Employment of Women] trials are to continue but are not to be regarded as trials, but as the lead-up or preparation for full integration, that is, the CREW exercise will be the first stage of implementation of a new policy of full integration of women into all units and occupations now closed to them.*

- *Full integration is to take place with all due speed, as a matter of principle and as a matter of practice, for both the active and reserve forces.*

- *The implementation of the principle requires the removal of all restrictions from both operational and personnel consider-ation; the minimum male requirement should be phased out; new occupational personnel selection standards should be imposed immediately.*

- *There must be internal and external monitoring of the policy with appropriate modifications being made immediately.*

- *The CAF and Canadian Human Rights Commission are to devise a mutually acceptable implementation plan so that the integration of women proceed[s] steadily, regularly and consistently toward the goal of complete integration of women within the next ten years.*

In a message to all members of the Forces dated March 1989 explaining the decision, General Paul D. Manson, the Chief of the Defence Staff, stated that it

can be looked upon as the latest (and presumably the last) of a series of develop-ments within the CF over the past 20 years leading to the establishment of full equality between men and women of the forces... Full integration is now the law of the land and we must obey the law... It is up to all of us to make it work, in a true spirit of equality.

Captains Jane Foster and Deanna Brasseur, two of the first women to train as fighter pilots, standing on the engines of a CF-18 at CFB Cold Lake, 20 June 1989. (CFPU, CKC 89-3773)

Implementing the Decision, 1989–91

At the outset, all occupations (with the two exceptions noted above) were immediately opened to women. The process used was determined by the plans for the CREW trials. All policies that had previously governed the employment of either men or women in specific areas were re-written, and the Directorate of Women Personnel was disbanded. This move was seen as "a positive step in the normalization of the employment of women as it is now a matter of normal procedure for staffs involved in the formulation of plans and policies to take into consideration the reality of the mixed-gender composition of the CF."

The "right to serve" in all occupations and all units of the Forces also brought with it a "liability to serve" for women who may have joined under the old regulations. A statement dated July 1989 reinforced the meaning of the new policies and stressed that "all members of the regular force are at all times liable to perform any lawful duty under terms and conditions as prescribed by the CDS [Chief of the Defence Staff]" notwithstanding the "policies in effect at the time of enrolment." Servicewomen who had enlisted during the period in which they were not required to participate in field units were suddenly confronted with a new reality. It was not always a welcome reality — the first report of the Minister's Advisory Board on Women in the CF noted that senior naval servicewomen resented the "liability to serve at sea" and that women who had traditionally been posted with static units and bases possibly did not have the requirements to succeed in a field unit.

Having all occupations open to them did not necessarily mean that women would enter the non-traditional ones or that they would be successful in these new roles. Servicemen and women alike complained about the "inability of some women, particularly in support roles, to complete efficiently occupation-specific field tasks." Others noted that women who failed caused problems for their female colleagues, who were "painted with the same brush" as the "unqualified, unfit and/or unmotivated." Those women who proved incapable of carrying out the new tasks grew increasingly demoralized as their shortcomings became evident.

Private Heather R. Erxleben, Canada's first female infantry soldier, and Private Dan J. Lagasse dug in a defensive position during a field exercise with 3 Battalion, Princess Patricia's Canadian Light Infantry, 26 March 1989. (CFPU, IXC 89-065)

Captain Karen Dunford during a mine clearance exercise at CFB Chilliwack, 15 March 1989. (CFPU, IXC 89-53)

Private Nikol Hock, a member of 2 Military Police Platoon, talking on a field radio during Exercise RIGHT CHOOSE in the Borden-Meaford area, 30 April 1990. (CFPU, IOC 90-8-1)

Lieutenant Monroe, a nurse with 2 Field Ambulance, firing a riot (CS Gas) gun during Exercise OSONS CHALLENGE at CFB Petawawa, 27 October 1988. (CFPU, ISC 88-993)

Between the time of the CHRC decision in 1989 and March 1991, a total of 20 women enrolled as combat arms officers (infantry, artillery or armour). Nine failed or withdrew and 11 continued their training. Again, the Minister's Advisory Board noted some of the problems that had occurred. Female candidates in the first group at the Princess Patricia's Canadian Light Infantry Battle School in Wainwright, Alberta, lacked the requisite physical strength and endurance. This could be attributed, according to the Board, to the fact that during the period immediately after the opening of combat arms to women "entry standards were reduced or waived in order to achieve the 'critical mass' necessary to provide, it was believed, social support for the female infantry candidates. All but one of these female recruits failed."

The concept of critical mass — that a minimum number of women are required for success — has been central to the discussion of gender integration in the CF, particularly in the land and sea environments. The designation of certain units as "mixed-gender units" was intended to "integrate women into those units and occupations from which women were previously barred in a way that will cause the least disruption to the individuals involved." Personnel staff intended that more units would be designated mixed-gender once "the number of women within critical MOCs [Military Occupations] increase sufficiently to make designation of additional units and ships feasible." This critical mass-based plan was approved by the CHRC.

The recruit school at Cornwallis, Nova Scotia, tested women against a lower fitness standard and found that they were simply not prepared. An additional problem was the decision to send servicewomen to battle schools as part of a critical mass, which often meant that the time lapse between their initial training and their arrival at battle school was unnecessarily long. As a result, while men moved from basic training to battle school as a group, these women became separated from colleagues with whom they may have formed allegiances. Finally, allegations were made relating to "significant peer harassment."

The Advisory Board reported that reaction to integration was uneven across the country. At Canadian Forces Base Petawawa senior officers and senior NCOs did not resist integration but apparently did little to ensure its success. Opinions differed on whether women were able to meet the standards of the combat arms, but, as there were no women serving in the combat units at Petawawa, these opinions continued to be based on speculation.

At CFB Gagetown the atmosphere was generally more supportive, as this base had experience in the training of women. At 1 Canadian Brigade Group in Calgary, some units were beset by an atmosphere that was "hostile, both between genders and toward the system." The Advisory Board found that some servicemen seemed to believe that "the elements of CREW are still on trial and that a case can be built to challenge or appeal the Tribunal decision."

The brigade commander presented an extensive list of concerns, including the perception that women lacked the physical fitness to carry out their duties, thus obliging men to work harder; were less aggressive than men, thus undermining overall effectiveness and safety; and were simply not motivated. In

Members of a refuelling team in Bahrain, 1991. (CFPU, ISC 91-5235)

addition, there were problems relating to the staffing needed to cover pregnancy leaves and the tendency of male personnel to become overly protective of their pregnant colleagues. Finally, while the overall effect on cohesion was thought to be neutral, the brigade commander noted that some members believed the order to integrate was wrong but carried it out nonetheless, although they felt betrayed by their leaders.

To facilitate the transfer of women into the "new" officer classifications, the naval reserve training system offered a "conversion course" for women who had qualified in the more traditional fields; this allowed them to switch into the equivalent year of training in the newly opened fields. Such compromises could not make up for the fact that men who had begun their training in the maritime surface and sub-surface courses frequently had more seagoing experience than newly transferred servicewomen.

The conventional wisdom is that having a significantly large group of women proceed through the system together will reduce the "fish bowl" effect of having too small a group and will build natural support systems. There is apparently some truth to this, as women in combat-arms training or other non-traditional environments in otherwise all-male peer groups reported a variety of problems, including "fear of aggression from male peers, extreme social isolation, and perceptions of a disproportionate day-to-day workload with no peers to assist with cleaning duties, etc." They acknowledged that some of their male colleagues provided social and moral support but maintained that their experience would have been less of a trial if they had had the company of other women. Yet some women described situations of competing against, rather than supporting, female colleagues. It may be that a shift in traditional preconceptions and biases towards servicewomen will require a critical mass large enough to affect the CF as a whole.

As women gradually entered new occupations they ushered in a number of "firsts." Those women who volunteered for the CREW trials under the CHRC ruling became leaders in several fields, and once the trials became the first phase in the implementation of full integration, these participants gained a greater sense of security from knowing that no future decision could disqualify them from their chosen occupation.

These women were often the focus of attention, not only from the media but also from their male colleagues. Being in the spotlight quickly lost its appeal, however, as Leading Seaman Susan Gencarelli told *Sentinel* magazine: "I didn't want to be centred out for attention. I just wanted to be treated as an equal." Ordinary Seaman Cheryl Whalen echoed the sentiment: "I don't want to be the first at anything anymore," she remarked, "I just want to be me — to get on with my career." Major Deanna Brasseur explained that the interest shown in the first woman to enter a particular field "not only created a chasm between her and her male colleagues, but led people to make a distinction between her performance and that of her co-workers."

Brigadier-General Sheila Helstrom, Canada's first female general officer, acknowledged in a *Sentinel* interview that the spotlight forced her into a dual role: as an officer and as a role model. In Helstrom's opinion, though, she was "just another officer

Captain Deanna Brasseur, one of the first women
to train as a fighter pilot, kneeling in front of a CF-18,
22 March 1989. (CFPU, ISC 89-118)

Captain Jane Foster, kneeling in front of a CF-18,
22 March 1989. (CFPU, ISC 89-117)

who has worked hard and has had a very rewarding career." She noted that there are "other women in the military who are also breaking ground, and the scrutiny they are under puts an awful lot of pressure —

Captain Jane Foster at CFB Cold Lake, 22 March 1989. (CFPU, ISC 89-117)

extra pressure — on them. In a way it's unfair but it's something we have to live with for now."

A Period of Financial Retrenchment, 1992–96

In 1992 the federal government announced plans to eliminate the deficit, and the Department of National Defence (DND) shifted its focus to budget cuts and reorganization. At the same time the CF became involved in a number of major peacekeeping missions abroad. While in this context gender integration progressed, it appears to have received a much lower priority.

There were other pressures on the progress of integration in the Forces during this period. The end of the Cold War brought with it the common perception that there was no longer a need for strong military forces, a perception that harmonized nicely with government fiscal policy and led to budgetary retrenchment and personnel reductions. Recruiting levels were cut and the traditional areas of women's service — administration and support — were restricted in favour of combat-related occupations, while the number of people offered re-enlistment at the end of limited terms of service was also cut back.

The perceived need to shrink the Canadian military establishment fostered the military equivalent of early retirement. The Force Reduction Programs, offered to non-commissioned members from 1992 to 1996 and to officers from 1994 to 1996, had the desired effect: by 1998, the numbers of both women and men in the regular force were lower than they had been in 1989. During these years of downsizing the representation of women improved because, proportionately, a greater number of men left the forces.

Yet positive steps were also taken during this period. In the light of a survey of harass-

Rifle above head (CFPU)

ment that appeared in 1992, and in consultation with the CHRC, the CF adjusted their harassment policies and practices, established an anti-harassment office and created a mandatory training program, the Standard for Harassment and Racism Prevention (SHARP). Matters such as family responsibilities and conditions of service, which previously had been identified as "women's issues," were now increasingly treated as general personnel policy. New maternity benefits were brought into effect, and parental leave — available to either spouse for up to 10 weeks — was introduced.

It became clear that harassment awareness and prevention programs could have unintended negative effects. As the Minister's Advisory Board reported in 1994, some male members of one infantry unit referred to the harassment prevention course as "The Threat" or "The Lethal Briefing," while female members believed they were "avoided by the more apprehensive men for some time thereafter." While harassment may have been curbed, the disruption to the cohesion of this unit clearly signalled the need for a different approach and for sensitivity to the potential for disruption. Concerned about being charged with harassment, some NCOs hesitated to discipline female soldiers, leading a number of male soldiers to conclude that women were receiving preferential treatment.

Each of the Minister's Advisory Board reports for the first five years of integration identified matters requiring attention. In its mid-term review, the Board congratulated National Defence Headquarters for its response to complaints concerning operational and non-operational clothing for servicewomen. Even so, they criticized the CF for taking so long to acknowledge "the issue of clothing and equipment and to commit to solving long-identified concerns in this regard."

In reference to kit problems — equipment and uniforms — women were not alone in their complaints. Not everyone is "average," and both small and large men found items such as the rucksack uncomfortable because it had been designed for a medium-sized man. Other complaints related specifically to the uniforms issued to women. On the premise that they were intended to present a "professional, disciplined look that is functional," the Advisory Board recommended that "women's uniforms should not be designed to ensure that female serving members look like 'ladies,' or 'nicer' than men; nor should their uniform design sacrifice functionality to emphasize (de-emphasize) body shape." Dress policy should be influenced not by gender differences, they argued, but by differences in body shape. The Canadian Forces Clothing and Dress Committee investigated complaints regarding the fit, quality, size range, design and fabric of uniforms. Where complaints were deemed legitimate, trials of redesigned clothing were undertaken and new items adopted. This process continues today, and the army "Clothe the Soldier" program is paying particular attention to the needs of female members as part of a general review.

In 1994 a nine-point plan, named MINERVA after the Roman goddess of war and wisdom, was developed to increase the overall participation of women in the Forces. Its elements included the following:

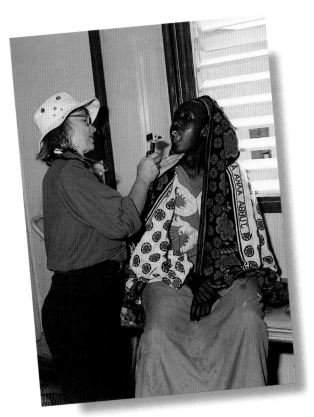

Lieutenant (N) Mackinnon of HMCS *Preserver*
examining a Somali woman during Operation
DELIVRANCE, January 1993.
(CFPU, HSC 92-849-261/262)

Peacekeepers with Cambodia Mine Action Team visiting an orphanage, 1992.
(CFPU, ISC 92-1199)

- *reaffirm the commitment by senior leaders regarding employment equity;*

- *gender awareness training;*

- *conduct analyses of trends concerning women (systematic barriers, release, enrolment, IPS [indefinite period of service] offers, PER [personnel evaluation report] rating comparison, rank progression comparison, awards nominations);*

- *target certain women in business and other government departments to hold honorary appointments.*

This plan had less of an impact than expected, and in a number of areas real events surpassed the theoretical goals. By 1997 progress had been made, although it is not clear whether this was a direct result of the plan.

Peacekeper with Cambodia Mine Action Team holding a toy destined for an orphanage, 1992.
(CFPU, ISC 92-1155)

- *provide greater geographical stability;*

- *facilitate discharge of family obligations;*

- *modify recruiting methods;*

- *ensure key position posting available for women, including specialist;*

- *encourage monitoring at all levels;*

Prioritization of Gender Integration, 1996–99

Between 1996 and 1999 gender integration once again became a priority for the CF as they prepared to address the necessary changes in culture and attitude that would supplement fair application of policies and practices. One example of the shift in attitudes is the decision to count time taken for maternity and parental purposes as qualifying time for the Canadian Forces Decoration. Such leave is no longer counted as a medical condition but rather as a normal part of a military career.

A short-term program for special selection into the Canadian Forces Command and Staff College was instituted for female officers whose military careers had begun under the old system. Offering these women access to operational occupations in the midst of their careers required a number of concessions. In simple terms, some women were ineligible for staff college because early in their careers they had been ineligible for certain

Captain Eva Martinez, the first Canadian woman to serve as a United Nations Military Observer, and Major Paul Lansey during Operation VISION (Guatemala), 1997. (Courtesy of Paul Lansey)

Captain Eva Martinez and Major Paul Lansey pose with demobilized Guatemalan guerrillas during Operation VISION, 1997. (Courtesy of Paul Lansey)

occupations, and thus the requisite training. These women were now too senior to attend the courses and gain the required work experience. To allow for their participation, a separate merit list and three additional positions had to be created. This short-term catch-up program will eventually be phased out, since it does not apply to female officers who entered the Forces under the fully integrated system.

Many DND publications addressed the subject of gender integration, focusing, where possible, on successes. For example, an article in the May 1997 *Defence 2000 News-letter* discussed a number of improvements. Equipment such as the rucksack, combat clothing, gas mask and aircrew equipment had been modified to better fit women. Mess decks in ships had been reconfigured to provide living spaces for mixed-gender crews. Gender issues had been addressed in seminars, lectures and leadership packages, and identical recruiting selection standards had been promulgated for men and women. The Army Lessons Learned Centre published the volume *Lessons Learned — Leadership in a Mixed Gender Environment,* addressing cultural myths, how to determine whether fault lies with "gender" or "leadership," and a series of related subjects such as unit cohesion and discipline in the context of solid leadership characteristics.

The matter of sexual harassment was brought into focus in a very public way in the 25 May 1998 issue of *Maclean's* magazine. This story generated such a response that it was covered in three subsequent issues and was picked up by other national media. Thirty-one allegations of sexual misconduct were brought forward, and all were reviewed by the Canadian Forces National Investiga-

tion Service. As of December 1998 four cases were still under investigation, one had been reopened and 11 were considered closed because the alleged victims did not wish to pursue the matter or could not be identified. Another 11 had been investigated and judicially resolved, while three were closed without charges being laid. Only one investigation resulted in charges being laid. The Chief of the Defence Staff, acknowledging that harassment problems had not been properly handled in the past, established a toll-free telephone number for the relay of information about possible incidents.

Stereotype and Reality: The Gulf War and Peacekeeping

Throughout its history, the Canadian military, in common with armed forces around the world, has struggled to bring together two cultures: that of the society it serves and that which it has nurtured over the years. The CF can change its practices and influence the attitudes of its personnel to some extent, but recruits bring their own attitudes and perceptions that may reflect neither Canadian attitudes of tolerance and understanding nor the military's commitment to the creation of a fully gender-integrated service. A recent DND study concluded:

The attitudes underlying gender harassment are grounded in obvious gender differences and lifelong socialization. They form a part of the latent stereotypes shared by both men and women in society. Basic training instructors have noted that many male recruits enter the CF with these attitudes fully formed and that vigilance is required to prevent peer harassment from occurring within mixed gender platoons. They can suppress the behaviour of these individuals,

Sergeant Sheila Hiscock on patrol duty around HQ CANFORME in Manama, Bahrain, as part of Canada's Gulf War forces, 12 January 1991. (CFPU, ISC 91-4124)

Persian Gulf during the Gulf War. These women served in the Gulf region from August 1990 through April 1991 in one of the Canadian operations — SCIMITAR (Air), FRICTION (Naval), ACCORD (Headquarters) or SCALPEL (Medical) — as integrated components of their units.

Administrative orders were issued to help the women adapt to the customs of the Arab states in which they were posted. The 39 women of the 550-member Canadian Air Task Group Middle East were counselled that if they left the military base "they would have to wear dresses extending from the neck to the ankles, with sleeves to the wrists. They would have to be escorted in public and were never to offer their hand when meeting Arab men. Also, they could not drive cars." Other

but the basic prejudice remains. It takes very little to reinforce such stereotypes and continuous control of discriminatory behaviour is necessary.

One way to combat the stereotyping of a group is to demonstrate the competence of that group. The CF have learned a great deal about women in service through their active participation, not only in peacekeeping missions but also in the Gulf War.

Prior to 1990, policy had largely prevented women from serving in the Middle East because of the cultural barriers erected by the host societies. Shifting circumstances caused staff to send women with the various elements of the CF posted to the

Personnel from HMCS *Preserver* carrying sandbags to the Canadian Embassy in Mogadishu, Somalia, during Operation DELIVRANCE, January 1993. (CFPU, HSC 92-849-32)

women deployed in the Persian Gulf were bound by similar restrictions.

Approximately 150 naval women served at the in-theatre headquarters and on board HMCS *Protecteur,* with no reports of incidents relating to the mixed-gender environment. The ship's company and observers noted that the presence of women seemed to have a "calming influence," perhaps because a mixed unit more closely resembles normal life. Seventy women, part of the land force contingent of 575 stationed in Qatar, served in headquarters and in the 1st Canadian Field Hospital, and after the war a further six women from a combat engineer regiment worked with their male colleagues "to clear mines and unexploded shells to establish a safe patrol route through the demilitarized zone on the Iraq–Kuwait border."

During their Gulf service, women reported that the small controversies relating to interpersonal relations between service men and women "disappeared, [as] personnel became more task-oriented and personnel were able to form cohesive groups more readily as a result of active duty." Of the 3,500 regular and reserve force personnel deployed to the Gulf, 240 — or seven per cent — were women. A 1994 NDHQ report stated that the servicewomen were "fully integrated in the Canadian contingent and did not demand, require, or receive any special consideration."

Canadian servicewomen have also served as peacekeepers in places as diverse as Cyprus, the Golan Heights, Sinai, Namibia, Honduras, Pakistan, Western Sahara, Cambodia, Somalia, the former Yugoslavia, Guatemala and Haiti. They have served in combat, combat support and combat service support roles on land, in supply ships, in tactical helicopter squadrons and in seagoing helicopter detachments. Reserve force women have joined their regular force counterparts on these missions, often as the only woman in a platoon or company.

These peacekeepers have faced challenges in their work. Some have complained of being excluded from operations or having their "in-theatre employment restricted as the result of a commander's attitudes, beliefs or preferences. Indeed, requests for exclusion [are] occasionally still received [in 1995] when a new commander is posted into these theatres." Others report that even though they might accompany their unit on the front line, they are sometimes assigned less demanding tasks or sent to rear areas if they express discomfort. A perceived need to protect women has often been raised by men in units that have had little or no experience of working with them. To a great extent, the servicewomen themselves influence how they are perceived; the female member who appears self-confident is treated as an equal, while one who appears fright-ened or self-conscious might find herself isolated.

The diverse cultures of countries that collaborate on United Nations and other international missions also affect the work of Canada's female peacekeepers. Canadian servicemen with little experience of working with women might fear that their foreign partners will ridicule or refuse to deal with female members of the military. Women who have served in multinational forces report that they are sometimes "tested" or ignored but are generally able to complete their tasks. They have requested education on the culture of their host country and on the forces they will be serving alongside. They have also identified a need for information about the environmental and physical conditions they are likely to encounter in-theatre, as well as "clothing requirements, ablution facilities and the availability of personal hygiene supplies."

Master Corporal Linda Chassé of the Royal 22e Régiment Battle Group transport section, 17 September 1992. (CFPU, ISC 92-5821)

Progress and Problems, 1989–99

Convincing women to join the military is only one of the challenges of creating a gender-integrated force. Getting them to stay in the CF long enough to become eligible for promotion within the NCO and officer ranks

is another. Servicewomen of all ranks still tend to leave at higher rates than their male counterparts. The reasons for this attrition rate vary and may reflect a blend of motivations. Sexual harassment and discrimination have certainly shaped the decision of many to take their release, while for others it has been the lack of properly fitting and appropriately designed kit. The conflicts inherent in balancing family life with a military career also appear to affect women more than men, especially those serving in the field or at sea. Testifying before the Standing Committee on National Defence and Veterans' Affairs, Master Corporal C. Gelsinger described the process that determined whether she and her military husband would serve at the same location. As he held a higher rank, his career manager would find him a posting and then speak with her career manager, who would then present her with the proposed arrangement. Each time, Corporal Gelsinger felt it was a case of "take it or leave." She objected not to the overseas postings or courses that kept her apart from her husband, but to the breaking of promises to keep them together on a day-to-day basis. It was rumoured on her base, and others, Corporal Gelsinger testified, that failure to co-locate married service members was a new force-reduction plan.

Accommodation in a mixed-gender environment presents a challenge when members are required to interact outside the "normal work day." In an operational or training situation, for example, "all members must have equal access to orders, instructions, and information on virtually a 24-hour basis, which is difficult when accommodation is segregated by gender." The Minister's Advisory Board recommended that a principle of "proximity and privacy" be followed in order to keep women "in the loop" as much as possible while ensuring privacy for members of both sexes. As a result, personnel staff planners have tried to ensure that unit cohesion is not weakened and informal learning is not interrupted because women are housed separately, at the same time defusing complaints that women are receiving special treatment by being accommodated in separate quarters. In field units, a curtained-off area in a main tent and a schedule for ablutions can address privacy needs. On board ship, the Advisory Board noted, where space is constrained and all-female mess decks are the norm, integration proves more difficult. "Inevitably, female crew members may be left 'out of the loop' through separation from the division or detachment while others may have essential career training delayed because billets are not available." Leading Seaman Susan Gencarelli, in an interview published in *Sentinel,* complains of being isolated from the male stokers' (marine engineers') mess deck. "When the stokers get together, we're left out," she says. "We miss a lot because of that. When I was doing my training, I did a lot of it by myself because I couldn't just sit down in the mess deck and talk it out with the other stokers."

Throughout the process of gender integration, servicewomen have faced prejudice based on the false impression that quotas require the enrolment of a specific number of women in certain occupational areas. This widespread misunderstanding obscures the reality that the best candidates are sought, regardless of their sex.

Despite these problems, the CF has made progress. By 1999 the number of women in senior officer ranks had increased, although the number in junior officer ranks had declined. Since recruiting in general had in fact been largely curtailed in the preceding decade, the number of men in these ranks also decreased. A similar pattern was seen within the ranks of non-commissioned

Sergeant Georgia Sheppard, instructor trainee at CFB Cornwallis, May 1988. (CFPU, IHC 88-12-2)

members, although the gender balance among senior NCOs was much closer. The rate of female representation — that is, the number of women compared to the number of men at a particular rank — tells a greater

Members of the Communications Branch wearing a maternity smock, CFS Leitrim, November 1989. (CFPU, REC 90-1292)

success story when the numbers for 1989 and 1998 are examined. At each officer rank there was a growth in the percentage of women, and this was also true for non-commissioned members at all ranks except corporal and private. However, the lack of a critical mass of a cadre of officers and NCOs, both male and female, whose only experience is serving in a gender-integrated environment, appears to have mitigated against true gender integration.

The 10-year gender-integration program came to an end on 20 February 1999. All military occupational categories in the CF, except the submarine service and the Roman Catholic chaplaincy, were opened to women, and while there were few or no women serving in some of these categories, other areas demonstrated remarkable progress. In 1999,

for example, 28 per cent of first-year cadets at the Royal Military College were female, and women represented eight per cent of the hard-sea operator occupations. However, the overall increase in representation of women in the CF from 1989 through 1998 was less than one per cent. Policies have been reviewed and rewritten to reflect the changing role of women in society — in particular, the harassment policy was revised and strengthened and accommodation of matters relating to pregnancy and maternity/parental leave were formalized. The recruitment process was reworked and improved, both to make servicewomen more visible to potential recruits and to make the process gender neutral. Leadership and supervisory courses now routinely feature gender-awareness training. The need for equipment and clothing to meet the requirements of both men and women in terms of design and fit was also recognized, and physical standards were adjusted to be gender-free or gender-neutral. Finally, a great deal of investigation was undertaken to "determine the barriers, bias and progress of women in the CF."

While the CF was claiming success, the CHRC took a different view. In its opinion, "the Tribunal objectives have not been met." The Commission acknowledged that a number of positive steps had been taken but declared that it was "disappointed over the pace of integration." It pointed out that in 1989 women held one per cent of all combat positions, while the February 1999 data showed a figure of just over three per cent. By any definition of "full integration," the

Commission concluded, "these numbers demonstrate that it has yet to be achieved." The representation of women in senior positions and ranks also remained low, in the view of the CHRC, and because of restricted opportunities for promotion in many occupations — a result of downsizing — this situation may persist for the foreseeable future. The Commission cited a failure to persuade all members of the CF that men and women can work together in all environments, and it commented on the slow progress made in modifying equipment. The Commission also noted an absence of continuous effort to "identify and remove unnecessary barriers to women entering and staying in combat positions and the regular monitoring of results." Worse, in the Commission's opinion, although women formed only 11 per cent of the CF, they lodged 60 per cent of all harassment complaints.

Towards a New Century

While the driving force for gender integration in the CF was the CHRC, the need for women in the CF is no less real. According to the 1991 Census, women make up 28 per cent of that part of the population most likely to enlist. Given that the recruitable pool of males has been declining since the 1970s, attracting women to the Forces will become increasingly crucial. Demographic forecasts suggest that there is also a "political imperative" for the military to reflect the society which it serves and from which it is drawn. To that end, the different management and work styles of women can contribute new skills and experience to the

Canadian military. In attracting and retaining the best talent in a given field, the CF cannot discourage half the population or it will greatly reduce its pool of potential candidates. It is clear that demographics must be taken into account. A 1998 report by the Chief of Review Services argues that only when all personnel understand these non-tribunal motivators will a higher level of support for gender integration be achieved.

As a result of these considerations, the navy, army and air force have established recruiting goals for women, with the air force and navy developing additional plans to recruit and retain women. The air force has prepared *Partnerships for the Future,* a five-year plan intended to "identify and eliminate systemic barriers to the selection and success of women, thus ensuring that women will have full access to a satisfying and successful career in the Air Force — regardless of the career field or occupation that they choose." The air force has established a goal of recruiting women for up to 29 per cent of its strength, while the army has set a goal of 25 per cent.

However, since women are still four times more likely to leave the service than their male counterparts, they would constitute only seven per cent of the members in the army combat arms. The navy's plan, *VISION 2010 — The Integrated Navy,* provides for frequent review of "policy and practice through which women will be fully integrated within the Navy" and includes more than 30 research projects aimed at identifying possible systemic barriers and the "monitoring of gender integration activities." The navy has set its goal at 40 per cent, so that by the year 2010 female representation will be 25 per

Shoulder to Shoulder, Canadian Women's Army Corps poster.
(CWM - 56-05-12045)

cent. The discrepancy in numbers between the navy, army and air force is a result of varying rates of attrition among trained servicewomen. Crucial to the ultimate success of the recruitment and retention of women in the CF is the communication of the message, not only to servicemen but to society in general, that the military is setting targets, not quotas; that qualified servicewomen must be accepted as equals, not tokens; and that women are needed to meet staffing goals, not just political ones.

According to tradition, officers serve Christmas dinner to enlisted personnel, Daruvar, Croatia, 25 December 1992. (CFPU, ISC 92-6266)

CONCLUSION

The attention given to gender integration within the Canadian Forces in recent years should not obscure the fact that for more than a century Canadian women have served their nation in its time of need. Beginning in 1885, when women shared the same campaign hardships as male soldiers, and continuing through the Yukon Field Force and the South African War, the foundation of women's service has been the nursing tradition.

As international conflicts grew broader in scope during the 20th century, involving an increased commitment of national resources and a change in long-held beliefs, the role of Canadian women expanded from the traditional one to embrace other areas of military service. Although at first there was some reluctance to recruit them, women quickly proved themselves to be indispensable. By the end of the Second World War, just under 50,000 Canadian women had joined the Women's Royal Canadian Naval Service, the Canadian Women's Air Corps, the Royal Canadian Air Force (Women's Division) and the various nursing services.

Large-scale postwar demobilization in 1945–46 caused the demise of the three women's organizations, but an increasingly troubled international situation saw their re-establishment in the early Cold War period. The role and utility of military women came under scrutiny in the early 1960s, but a wave of social change leading to the legislated right of all Canadians, regardless of gender, to serve their country in uniform ensured a female presence in the three services and in their successor, the CF. The result has been an emphasis, over the past two decades, on full gender integration, and in this respect Canada has achieved an impressive record.

Progress, however, has not always been easy, as integration has had to overcome entrenched beliefs and enduring myths. Time will resolve many of the problems of full gender integration, and if recruitment remains steady or increases and attrition rates can be managed, "critical mass" may be achieved. When this happens, servicewomen will take their proper place, on an equal footing with servicemen, in the CF of the new century.

At present there is still room for improvement, but it would be all too easy to focus on the inequity that persists rather than on the progress that has been made. As Canadian society has adjusted its view of what constitutes suitable work for women, so too has the Canadian military. Apart from service in submarines and in the Roman Catholic chaplaincy, there are no barriers to women in the CF today. With a review currently under way that may end their exclusion from service in submarines, women might soon have complete access to all careers in the CF and, with time, can be expected to occupy all ranks and positions. The task before the leaders of the CF is to create an environment that will offer every possible opportunity to all Canadians who accept the exciting and rewarding challenge of a military career.

RELATED READING

Readers seeking more information could consult some of the following books on the experiences of women in the Canadian military. As a starting point, G.W.L. Nicholson's *Canada's Nursing Sisters* (Toronto: Samuel Stevens, Hakkert, 1975) tells the story of the earliest women to serve and brings the reader up to the point of unification. E.A. Landell, in *The Military Nurses of Canada: Recollections of Canadian Military Nurses* (White Rock, BC: Co-Publishing, 1995), has collected the memories of several nurses who served into the 1990s.

The Second World War has received by far the most attention from scholars. Ruth Roach Pierson's *"They're Still Women After All": The Second World War and Canadian Womanhood* (Toronto: McClelland & Stewart, 1986) examines the social changes — both real and imagined — that took place, while Jean Bruce's *Back the Attack! Canadian Women During the Second World War — at Home and Abroad* (Toronto: Macmillan, 1985) and Geneviève Auger and Raymonde Lamothe's *De la poêle à frire à la ligne de feu : la vie quotidienne des Québécoises pendant la guerre 39-45* (Montreal: Boréal-Express, 1981) offer insight into the daily lives of Canadian women during that period. Carolyn Gossage, in *Greatcoats and Glamour Boots: Canadian Women at War* (1939-1945) (Toronto: Dundurn, 1991), brings together the experiences of women in all branches of the military.

In addition to published secondary sources, compilations of the stories of women in a given area — often prepared and printed by a group of former servicewomen — are available in many local libraries. Museums and archives (particularly the National Archives of Canada and the Department of National Defence's Directorate of History and Heritage archives) also contain many military records, diaries and letters. Finally, the author was surprised at the large number of women who had spent all or part of their careers in the military and who were eager to share their stories.

INDEX

The page numbers in **bold type** refer to photographs.